Bill Clinton $5 Trillion surplus p.5

PERFECT TRAP

THE GOP'S 20 yr PLAN TO CAPTURE STATE, LOCAL & NATIONAL GOVERNMENTS FOR THE FORESEEABLE FUTURE

AND ADDITIONAL NOTES TO THE PRESIDENT FROM

1/21/12 THROUGH 9/23/12

BY

TURNIN A. HAUSROUND

JUSTICE BOOK PRESS

To the honor and the services of the extended

Joseph Biden family

In the past, present and the future

and, to the tranquil memory of the past.

Copyright @ 2012 by Justice Book Press

All rights to copies reserved and Liability Limited

Knowledge of or reading any part of this work limits Legal Liability of all kinds including tort/court to the maximum of total extent of a refund of the current price of the book or document only. This means the intender understands and agrees from the outset and knowledge of this work or book that there can be no initiation of any legal action, tort/suit against any entity associated with the writing, publication, printing or distribution of this work, book or document. Copies may be produced only by permission from the Author.

Printed in the United States of America

Designed by and Thoughts by the Author

Published by: Justice Book Press

USA

Library of Congress Cataloging - in - Publication Data

Hausround, Turnin A., PERFECT TRAP, DAMNED, Thoughts, President, Scourge, ReCorpiCON, History, Elections

PERFECT TRAP & Notes from 1/21/12 to 9/23/12 – 2nd ed.

A book by: JUSTICE BOOK PRESS

ISBN 978-1-300-09353-4

INTRODUCTION i

This book is THE absolute MUST READ to discover the Bottom Line Hidden Agendas of the ReCorpiCON party and how they set the PERFECT TRAP to take over the entire government, your entire lives – both GOP and Democrats, and reduce the taxes of the 1% to ZERO or NEAR ZERO. Keep in mind, Republicans, you will also be attacked by the middle class tax increases that will be required to pay for the huge tax reductions for the rich, huge increases in military spending & thus the funding of what is left of the government they intend to use to control every aspect of your lives for an eternity! They are shameless! You as GOP and Independents must defeat this TRAP they have set for you & foil their ReCorpiCON based Fascist plans & goals!

The GOP elite do not actually care for you except as VOTING FODDER to win the election for them so they can take over the government for generations to come! The details in this book, by design, have never been covered by the so called "Liberal Press" which turns out to be actually the "Corporate Press". This book will truly open your eyes to the "Why of the Why" of the ReCorpiCON' statements Versus the actions they're putting into place as you read this book! You think the nation in debt and you being subjected to a huge depression is an accident? Oh, think again! Think many times about this again and realize that this was a HUGE part of a plan to set a PERFECT TRAP to ensnare you and your EMOTIONS into falling for a "savior" to bring you out of the VERY ABYSS THEY CREATED TO SET THE PERFECT TRAP! And they actually have the BALLS to EXPECT you to thank them for destroying your very life and livelihood for a very extended, long time! You have got to stop being fooled by their constant propaganda and rationalizations that are designed to keep you feeling NEEDY & desperate for a change toward THE GOP!

ii   This is so <u>insidious & transparent</u> and <u>yet they are making it work RIGHT UNDER your eyes and noses so smoothly</u> that you fail to see it happening <u>as they boldly role it out before you</u>! Particularly, since 2010 when they felt so emboldened by wins in the House & the Senate that <u>they have not BEEN SHY</u> about passing the kind of nonsense legislations that SHOW TO THE WORLD WHAT KIND OF NONSENSE THEY ARE ACTUALLY ABOUT!

Stop and ask yourself the following question! Can you actually name ONE THING <u>THE GOP HAS DONE FOR YOU OR 'WE THE PEOPLE' DURING THE LAST 12 OR EVEN THE PAST 2 YEARS</u>? Think long and hard about that! Think very long and hard about this crucial question that <u>actually reveals the most about the aims and goals of the ReCorpiCON party and their minions</u>! Oh, lets count the TERRIBLE, HORRIBLE, AWFUL WAYS THEY HAVE DONE THINGS <u>TO YOU</u> THAT HAVE CAUSED TREMENDOUS PAIN AND SUFFERING TO YOU AND THE NATION AS A WHOLE! ACCIDENT?

There were two decade long, EXPENSIVE wars put on your, your children's and grand children's credit cards! There was the totally unpaid for, Medicare part D, an abomination in itself, that they lied about the cost to their own base to get passed in a two hour, middle of the night, ARM TWISTING beyond the vote cut-off time! There was the $3 trillion tax cut for the rich which they justified on a $5 trillion surplus generated by Bill Clinton and the Democrats in the previous administrations. They are now trying to continue to justify it in <u>these times</u> based on THE JOBS THAT THIS HAS OR WILL CREATE! WHAT A TOTAL FARSE! They imposed a <u>total abomination</u> on the educational prowess of America with "Every Child Left Behind" a deliberate attempt to dummy down America's main strengths! They have tried to <u>restrict voting rights all over America</u> in a "veiled attempt" to stop voter fraud. They have passed numerous laws to try to <u>stop unions and collective bargaining</u>! They are ANTI WOMEN and their very sacred rights by passing Vagina restrictive laws! Need I go on? I think you get the picture of the <u>PERFECT TRAP</u>!

TABLE OF CONTENTS iii

PREAMBLE AND PREFACE	1
CHAPTER 1	3
CHAPTER 2	5
CHAPTER 3	7
CHAPTER 4	9
CHAPTER 5	11
CHAPTER 6	13
CHAPTER 7	16
CHAPTER 8	18
CHAPTER 9	19
CHAPTER 10	21
SUMMARY OF WHAT WE HAVE LEARNED SO FAR	24
NOTE TO THE PRESIDENT 1/21/12	25
NOTE TO THE PRESIDENT 2/3/12	40
NOTE TO THE PRESIDENT 2/29/12	43
NOTE TO THE PRESIDNET 3/6/12	47
NOTE TO THE PRESIDENT 4/10/12	49
NOTE TO THE PRESIDENT 4/22/12	52
NOTE TO THE PRESIDENT 4/29/12	55
NOTE TO THE PRESIDENT 5/7/12	58
NOTE TO THE PRESIDENT 6/16/12	62
NOTE TO THE PRESIDNET 6/23/12	71
NOTE TO THE PRESIDENT 7/21/12	79
NOTE TO THE PRESIDNET 8/12/12	86
NOTE TO THE PRESIDENT 8/21/12	90
NOTE TO THE PRESIDNET 8/27/12	92
NOTE TO THE PRESIDENT 8/28/12	96
NOTE TO THE PRESIDENT 9/17/12	100
NOTE TO THE PRESIDENT 9/21/12	103
NOTE TO THE PRESIDENT 9/23/12	106

DEDICATION

To a Democracy that has been under attack

For an extended period of time

BY

Not just foreign terrorists – though important

BUT BY

Those, who, under the banner of Patriotism

Strive to create an enemy based upon fear

Of an uncertainty of future

THAT THEY, THEMSELVES

Have purposefully, successfully, created

And propagated in order to

Appeal to the emotions of fearful people

TO

Continue the Dastardly Deeds they have

CREATED

To capture the hearts and minds of a totally

SUPPRESSED, BURDENED

AND SUFFERING - WE THE PEOPLE.

PREAMBLE AND PREFACE

Looking at the picture on the face of the book, we see a pictorial representation of the GOP's plan for the PERFECT TRAP. The radial silk lines leading into the center are the actions that created the crisis and conditions that allow the GOP to ensnare voters on the concentric circular silks. They use them to turn disasters /economic hard times into needy voters "dependent" upon <u>their form of saving</u> to get them out of the trap. As we know with all traps, that is a totally useless & futile effort and the Black Widow spider (GOP) always wins. Unless we get smart and not venture into the trap in the first place. Never vote GOP ever again!

Lets look at the radial lines. One is Indifference. They use lack of transparency and lack of true concern for people as a means to make people feel needy and hopeless –in the dark and uninformed so dependent on them for info.

One is the unpaid for Medicare part D that will run up the debt a trillion dollars or more. That adds to the deficit that they tout as the reason that we have to have severe economic sanctions against the poor and middle class to fix the problems "that the Obama admin has created".

Two unpaid for wars has run the deficit up another 3trillion dollars. All deficits are thereby cited as being caused by the Obama Administration so they must be dealt with in a draconian manner. That makes people needy and desperate enough to believe anything they are told.

Taking $5 trillion, the Democrat's produced surplus, into a $10.7 trillion deficit "allows" them to argue that Obama is worthless and needs to be fixed/removed. Non believer!

2   A $3 trillion tax cut for the 5% has added another mile stone onto the deficit argument that we have to starve the government and screw it into the ground to survive! That reduction in govn will surely raise the unemployment index to over 10% further insuring a reason to blame Obama and his administration for the jobless problem!

Unregulation of energy companies that has led to the huge disasters in the Gulf by BP, Refinery explosions that killed 30 some employees and huge mine accidents in unregulated coal mines have caused a general concern about what Obama is doing to "ruin the freedom" of the energy industry. Therefore, these are all Obama's fault! We have slurry dams break flooding whole towns and near perfect scenic regions. We also have the raping of whole regions with open pit mines and fracking disasters all over the mid west that opens a whole can of worms!

Over the counter derivatives that were what ultimately crashed the entire US economy as well as a good part of the rest of the world led nicely to a GOP led opposition to Obama and corporate regulation. These were caused by the GOP deregulation of financial industry and Wall street.

Hubris, Hidden agenda and Secrecy kept the general public out of the real dealings of the GOP antics under VP Chancey and President Shrub. This means that they were able to pull off significant dirty dealings with energy, oil, reasons for war and bid-less contracts for Chancey's old company, Halliburton, and others that won hundreds of millions of dollar contracts with no bid process. Money for their buddies and close, rich, powerful GOP friends all at our Public expense and taxes <u>and on our credit cards</u>!

CHAPTER 01

The LOSS OF FAITH AND TRUST IN GOVERNMENT, rung

<u>The Americans are NOW believing</u> that the government is not only broke but that it needs draconian measures to CUT everything that everyone NEEDS out of the budget to save itself from total Failure. <u>GOP's huge Debt</u> has insured that they can sell the <u>Rationalization</u> that <u>the nation is at deaths door</u> and the only way to save it is to believe the ReCorpiCONs and <u>cut everything to the bone and then drown the critter</u>! This was <u>planned a generation ago & IS GOP agenda</u>! There is plenty of money to run the present government if the Rich would PAY the taxes they paid under Reagan & Corps would pay the taxes THEY OWE rather than ZERO they pay as the result of ReCorpiCON created loop holes & receiving subsidies for <u>No Reason</u>! <u>By Contrast,</u> <u>America's heyday and the American Dream was when highest tax rate was over 90% in 50's and 60's</u>!!

The deficit that <u>they, the ReCorpiCONs, created</u> was used to justify totally ideological grid locks that diminished the <u>Total Faith and Credit of the United States</u> and resulted in a CREDIT RATING DOWNGRADE FOR THE FIRST TIME IN THE HISTORY OF THE UNITED STATES!! Thank you, TeaBaggers. so <u>very God Damn much</u>!! You guessed it! <u>It also created a total downgrade of the faith and trust in the Federal government by We The People as well</u>!! Very Well Done!!

The ideological battles over the Debt Ceiling and funding of the government this summer took the Congressional <u>public opinion rating down to 9% > the lowest in history</u>!

4   Now, you might naively think that this would be a bad thing for the ReCorpiCONs and TBaggers! YOU WOULD BE WRONG! IT SERVED TO DESTROY AMERICA'S FAITH IN IT'S federal GOVERNMENT and thus it's usefulness to America! It defines the American Dream as coming from the GOP!!

The bottom line is that the Nation and the people in it WILL blame the present Administration and party for all of their woes, problems, turmoil, depressions, and difficulties that they are now experiencing and observing with the government. Dysfunctional operations are one of the KEY ISSUES the GOP CREATED that WOULD keep beating WE The People up & drive wedges to breed dissatisfaction!!

The ReCorpiCONs are counting on this fundamental belief that Americans will vote against their best interests by voting for "the so called ALTERNATIVE" to whatever or whom ever is in power at the moment! They are counting on the belief that you, America, will have forgotten the past and who actually created the problems that they are constantly pointing to as not being solved by the present administration or those in the House and Senate!

An interesting point might come to mind at this juncture! How did they know that Obama would win rather than John McCain? Why would they create such a disastrous situation assuming McCain might have won the election?

Odd as it may seem, the TOTAL BEAUTY of this scheme, hatched a generation ago, is that the TRAP would have been even more effective had McCain won! What, you say? Yes, the same arguments to diminish the size and spending of government would have worked even faster under McCain, as he'd have been a sympathetic SCHILL!

CHAPTER 02

The HUGE RECORD BREAKING DEFICIT, rung

Who'd guess a Record Breaking Deficit could be a useful tool the RecorpiCONs would use to entrap & get 99% of America to buy into & to do their bidding? Guess again!

Let's look at the facts before and after the tremendous election of Obama in 2008.

Fact 1. Bush Jr. started with a $5 trillion surplus provided by Democrat, Bill Clinton after Bush Senior left the country in total debt long before Bill Clinton took office.

Fact 2. GW Bush passed the Bush tax cut for the rich and wealthy BASED UPON THE PREMISE that we were more than solvent with a Democrat created $5 trillion surplus! We could then afford to give a $3 trill cut to the RICH!

Fact 3. The ReCorpiCONs left Obama with an ON THE BOOKS $10.7 trillion deficit before he even took office.

Fact 4. The ReCorpiCONs had charged another $3 trillion war debt on You and your Children and Grandchildren's credit cards that were not on the debt books left Obama. Obama, on his pledge for openness, put the war debt on the books >raising it to $13.7 trillion just after taking office!

Fact 5. The Bush ReCorpiCONs left another $1 trillion debt OFF THE BOOKS in the Medicare Part D bill passed in the middle of the night by lying to congress about the real cost of the bill and twisting the arms of Republicans for two hours past the stated time for closure of the vote.

6   When Obama, on his pledge for openness, put this hidden debt on the books the total was now $14.7 trillion.

Fact 6. With the country in the deepest depression since 1939, Obama pushed to have a $0.7 trillion Survival Bill passed to turn the economy around. The bill was very effective but WAS NOT LARGE ENOUGH to get the country back on track as fast as everyone needed it to be. This $0.7 trillion, ran the deficit up to $15.4 trillion which is where we find ourselves now! $0.7 divided by $15.7 is 5% of the total debt & doesn't even account for the $5 trillion surplus that Bush ran through before running up the Debt of Record! That makes Obama's contribution about 3.5%!

Why isn't this $20.7 trillion (ReCorpiCON SPENDING LIKE A DRUNKEN SAILOR DEBACLE) not an issue for the GOP's in 2010 or in 2012? WWII Germany total propaganda! That's why! They've taken a Madison Ave Branding, marketing approach of changing a Deficit (every Pun intended) into a Gross Huge ASSet - All other puns are intended as well!

Result: They blame the entire Deficit on Obama and say it often enough to make it stick with their dummied down, intelligence challenged followers! It's their focus and a battle cry of what is wrong with the Government and our present and future Dreams! They've made it the KEY ISSUE TBaggers repeat & have made it THE ISSUE taking away the punch from the real issues of the future of the United States: Education, Infrastructure, Manufacturing, Jobs and return to the American Dream like the 50' 60's. They've made it the DUMMY ISSUE to set the Perfect Trap! It is their TROJAN Horse they created to obfuscate the real Issues!

CHAPTER 03

The HIGH UNEMPLOYMENT rung of the PERFECT TRAP

<u>Creating, Keeping & Ensuring the Unemployment Index stays very high is a very powerful tool to further entrap the populace</u> on a number of very powerful levels to support the Greed Over People party's agendas and <u>for them to vote against their own best interests and benefits</u>!

What happens when you don't have a job or are in constant fear of losing yours?

The strong fears that you developed as a result of this causes you to become extremely upset with the present government and those who are at the "head of that government" – namely Obama! You "erroneously" blame them and him for:

1. Being the ones responsible for creating this high unemployment; (ABSOLUTELY & TOTALLY FALSE)

2. For seemingly doing nothing to reduce this index

3. Not being able to do anything about it, and

4. Not even seeming to try to do anything about it!

Well, as a result, this <u>populace that they have trapped</u> is led to think that their "savior" must have let them down! This Administration and, Yes, even the Democrats, have let them down and have betrayed the promises made during the campaign. THEREFORE, IMPLYING THAT THE ONLY "ALTERNATIVE" CONCLUSION IS TO VOTE FOR THE

8   ONES (WHO ACTUALLY CREATED AND WORKED TO MAINTAIN THE HORENDOUSLY HIGH UNEMPLOYMENT) TO COME BACK INTO POWER AND BAIL THEM OUT! Bull shit!

<u>That is like renting your attic to known firebugs and then buying them gas and matches in hopes of securing their TRUST that they'll SURELY appreciate your generosity</u>!

What happens when Unemployment remains high for a very long period of time?

Everyone is constantly concerned about lack of Jobs and possible Unemployment! What a perfect opportunity for every Energy Company in the USA to ramp up huge advertising campaigns about how the reduction or elimination of "terrible" regulations would free up and create 100's of thousands of high paying jobs in America! What a powerfully emotional message and what a powerful incentive for you, the populace, to consider voting for the Greed Over People Party – generally considered to be the anti regulation party – so that they will get in power, eliminate regulations and thus create 100's of thousands of jobs almost instantly! Powerful SHIT!

<u>Fear is a very powerful emotion and a powerful motivator to move people to do something that they will very soon clearly regret later</u>! Look at after affect of 2010 election! It also gives them a constant Mantra of "<u>Where's the Jobs</u>? Why isn't the (Obama) government doing something for Jobs? Ironically, <u>they blithely state that government can't do anything about creating jobs</u>! The private sector is the only entity that can do something about jobs. <u>In all this time, they have not written - passed one JOBS bill</u>! CRAP!

CHAPTER 04
The HUGE FORECLOSURE rung of PERFECT TRAP

<u>Fear, total fear, despair, fear and Hopelessness</u>! What an extremely powerful set of tools to create distrust, distaste, dissatisfaction, loathing, disrespect for the Government?

Oh My, who is this government now? It must be Obama and his "gang" of Pelosi, Reid, Schumer's, etc that are helping your lives go to hell so quickly! After all, the Bush government bailed out the Banks, (That did this to you) so you then ask, why isn't main street doing so much better now? After all, the stock market is doing well, and all of Wall Street got huge bonuses. Where is the bail out and huge bonuses for MAIN STREET? Who's stopping them?

The banks got bailed out, as well as rating agencies and insurance companies that created the Housing bubble that was allowed to grow unchecked as a result of the GOP removal of regulations that would have prevented the disastrous calamity that followed in 2006-2008!

What does this huge Foreclosure Riff do to your psyche?

It puts at least 10% of the population at <u>total risk</u> of not only losing the biggest investment made in their lives, but <u>puts their entire lives and ability to exist in total jeopardy</u>! What does that do to the cohesion of a family? Do you have any idea what a powerful affect that has on one's <u>sense of living the American Dream when you are living with children in a car or truck?</u> It makes them extremely vulnerable to what is going on in government – and of

10 course the government that gets blamed is <u>obviously the present government & those who are now in power!</u>

<u>What a beautiful TRAP to set for at least 10% of the entire population!</u> What a powerful tool to turn supporters of Obama; Democrats & Independents into angry – possibly anti Obama Democrats & Independents! <u>**WHAT A TRULY BEAUTIFUL TRAP TO SET BEFORE THE 2010/2012 ELECTIONS**</u>!

The Greed Over People party seems to think that they <u>can just play around</u> with our <u>lives</u> for purely political purposes as if <u>we are the 47% that they have written off & therefore really don't exist & simply don't matter</u>!!! Well it is actually more sinister than that. They planned this demise so that a lot of people will be put off by the situation they find themselves in during these critical times and will be ready and willing stooges to hear for a ReCorpiCON call for action to FIX THE PROBLEM BY THE VERY PARTY THAT GOT ALL OF US INTO THIS CRISIS.

Well, they will find that <u>we do matter</u>! That's why it's called Government By and For the People. <u>We are the people</u>!! And it is time for WE THE PEOPLE to start to matter and start voting EVERY ReCorpiCON out of office and make it stick for a very long time. Then the Government will again begin to work. With only a few GOP in office, nothing works for WE THE PEOPLE any more! They have a dozen think tanks working on how to game the Democracy/Republic System so it either doesn't work or only works for Corporations and the Rich at the very extreme expense of the very real WE THE PEOPLE!

<u>The Greed Over People Party has all the "answers" and knows that everyone will forget who STUCK IT TO THEM</u>!!

CHAPTER 05

The GLOBAL ECONOMIC INSTABILITY Rung

Sometime, a generation ago, ReCorpiCONs recognized that there was a <u>ton of money</u> that a lot of good, decent, hard working people had amassed by hard work and had saved and put into investments (retirements, houses, savings, banks, stocks, etc.) that needed to be RIPPED OFF!!!! So processes were developed to RIP OFF ALL of what was left of that discretionary money that these decent hard working people had earned over a lifetime for their enjoyment and future retirements. <u>Trumped up wars, for example took the money of not only us but our children, grand children and great grand children so easily it was like taking candy from a baby</u>!!! Building the housing bubble derivative swap markets took almost everything else not only here but also in the entire world.

Corporate influence has dictated that the rest of us will be <u>ripped off one way or the other</u> in terms of the loss of our precious resources taken without paying royalties while destroying our environments, property values and living conditions. When we are inundated with rising seas, <u>we will begin to realize how far they would go to destroy us and our lives</u> for their <u>Greed Over People agendas</u>!!!!

The bankrupting of All of America after the initial wars <u>rip off</u> was finalized with the planned and <u>bet upon housing bubble collapse</u> followed by a near collapse of the world banking and financial markets. That global collapse has manifest itself in near collapses of governments like Italy, Greece, Ireland & Spain. The "prescribed solution" there by their <u>ReCorpiCON elements is a total draconian</u>

12   _austerity of government services_. You think it was an accident? Think again! Why do the ReCorpiCONs keep pointing to Greece with such _gusto and Glee_? They are using it as a _club_ to _beat you into submission to follow their line of fear and panic to do their bidding_!! The real solution should've been a greater tax paid by the _richest and corporations paying their fair share of taxes for the tremendous financial benefits they all reaped quiet bountifully as a result of controlling the government and tax revenues to pay for the services that were provided_.

Did you not know that the ZENITH of the '50-'60's built East/West & North/South super highways across this huge country? _Great Public Funded Universities_ trained an _elite FORCE_ of scientists, engineers, managers and financial experts that built Silicon Valley, Science Triangle in the SE & Rt 128 in Mass. Great _expanding_ high tech companies like Tektronix, Hewlett Packard, Google, Apple, Micro Soft, Intel, Lockheed, Sylvania, Boeing, Martin Marietta, Sarnoff, General Electric, McDonnell-Douglas, etc. were all _huge beneficiaries of an extensive, publically funded_ higher education/research university complex. _They all benefited immensely from huge Government contracts_. These and 1000's of more high tech companies _derived huge advantages over the rest of the world_ by this great system of publically funded infrastructures. These were built from +90% and corporate taxes that paid 45% of the government expenses. _Now that they've all made great fortunes from these extremely necessary advantages, they seem to forget their roots and no longer feel a need to fund them and 1000's of other beneficial programs that government supplied for their common good_! THE TRAP!!!!

CHAPTER 06

LOSS OF ESSENTIAL JOBS & SERVCS - STATE & LOCAL LEVEL

With the <u>deliberate collapse</u> of the entire Fed. Economy came the <u>also intended consequences</u> of the collapses of State and Local economies. Now the obvious question most would ask is; "why would any organized group or party <u>deliberately sink the economies of states</u>, counties or cities"? I'll try to put the <u>BEST SPIN</u> on a totally illogical agenda of a totally depraved group or ideology. (Greed Over People) Party, tends to believe that the <u>best way to save the Republic</u> is to <u>take everyone down</u> (except the elite few at the top) <u>to correct</u> gradual long term inflation <u>in one giant step backwards</u> to lower all salaries, savings, discretionary & direct spending <u>to an almost poverty level</u>. <u>To them, this is the ultimate patriotism</u> by <u>resetting</u> the <u>norm to worldwide third world POVERTY levels</u>. If you do not believe this, just read their nearly hidden agenda statements that you might be able to obtain from some of your GOP friends. The TeaParty is not shy about sharing these agendas. They are just "<u>DAMNED</u>" proud of them!

Now, let's get to the <u>real reason</u> for this <u>deliberate action</u> and why it is so <u>important to them to set the Perfect TRAP</u>!

Ask yourself, who is most hurt by the collapse of the local economies? Is it the rich, the middle class or the poor? <u>It is the middle class and the poor!</u> Not only do they have the <u>first direct hit</u> (a form of tax) by loss of salaries, jobs and even housing but <u>they get a double whammy</u> when those cities, counties and yes the state are forced to cut back on essential services that take away whatever support they had left to cope with their new, disastrous

14   situations. THEIR SUPPORT STRUCTURE SIMPLY DROPS OUT FROM UNDER THEM. THEY END UP <u>PAYING TWICE FOR THE ACTIONS OF THOSE AT THE TOP</u> THAT DELIBERATELY BROUGHT THIS HOLLOCAUST UPON THEM! Look at this equation! When the rich end up making much more as the result of these deliberate actions, the <u>middle class and poor end up PAYING TWICE</u> for the dire situations they find themselves in <u>as no fault of their own!</u> <u>THE TRAP!</u> This is a <u>ZERO SUM GAME</u>! Rich pay less> Poor pay more!

<u>Now stop and think of the total inequality of this injustice!</u> What is affected at the state and local levels? Education, schools, social services, food stamps, welfare, senior tax deferrals, police, fire depts. and unemployment services! Do any of these really affect the rich if at all? No, but <u>they stomp the hell out of what the poor and middle class</u> rely upon <u>to survive in tough times</u>! This is crucial to <u>THE TRAP!!</u> So why does the (Greed Over People) party so strongly insist that the <u>rich not only pay no higher taxes</u>, but rather want to lower them to almost zero. Again, a ZERO SUM GAME! IF THE RICH PAY LESS, MIDDLE CLASS HAS TO TAKE UP THE DIFFERENCE OR GO WITHOUT ALMOST ALL THAT THEY HAD COME TO RELY UPON OVER THE PAST 60 YEARS! Do you now think that in all fairness, the rich need to pay a HELL OF A LOT MORE now for GROSS sins of their GREED? Hey, that's a no brainer! You're <u>DAMNED</u> right on this one!

As bad and as obvious all this tends to be, we must now deal with how all of this misery and <u>poverty sets and springs the PERFECT TRAP</u> the (GREED OVER PEOPLE) party started setting for you well over a generation ago!

The <u>TRAP</u> is the newly imposed poverty on the MC!   15
Desperation, desperation, desperation breeds a <u>terrible sense of need to be "saved" by someone</u>! Let me say that again!! Desperation, desperation, desperation breeds a terrible need to be "saved" by someone! Oh let me guess! Would it be "SATAN", as the church lady often said? <u>DAMNED</u> right! Just the ReCorpiCON governors and ReCorpiCON state houses that took over in response in 2010 to the frustration the nation found itself in as the <u>direct result of the GREED OVER PEOPLE's party actions in the past decade</u>. It's like being beat up by a street gang and out of the dark shadows, the gang leader comes out and says to you; "This looks like police brutality to me". I know the best way out of this tragedy". I will be your leader out of your mess & <u>promise a better life for you</u>! And YES, THAT IS THE "<u>PERFECT TRAP</u>"! <u>The dumb fall for it</u>!

Let me give you a real example of the DOUBLE WAMMY that has occurred in some states as a direct result of the deliberately caused financial crisis. Many senior citizens had a "covenant" with their states that they could defer their property taxes until they died or sold the house. After the financial crisis, the state suddenly changed the "covenant" so that some 20K seniors no longer qualified for the deferral of property taxes. That meant that all of a sudden they had to start paying those taxes – something their budgets could not tolerate. In a few cases, there were delinquent taxes that were deferred as long as they were eligible for the state funded deferral. If that deferral was canceled, <u>all delinquent taxes became due</u>! That meant $ 20,000 was <u>due immediately or foreclosure</u>! <u>THE TRAP</u>! <u>We have all been victims of the GOP PERFECT TRAP</u>!

CHAPTER 07

TREMENDOUS ANXIETY AND FEAR OF FUTURE

After all that has already been said, this one seemingly is a no brainer! However, there are subtleties that must be exposed completely. By deliberately causing the crash that we all find ourselves in, the ReCorpiCONs set in force a path to ensure the total take over of all governments in the United States, Federal, State, County and Cities for the next foreseeable future. With the horrendous financial distress that has been deliberately imposed upon these United States, there develops a tremendous anxiety for 99% of people in the United States. If you lost your job, you fear that you will never be able to get a new one if even at a much lower salary than you had before. If you still have a job, you're in constant fear that you may lose it sometime soon! Running on a marginal budget just to get by, the prospect of stoppage of income becomes a tremendous stressor. Most people cannot survive more than a few weeks to a month or two. To be much worse, if you have lost your house, you are under tremendous stress as to how you & your family may be able to get by.

How does this boil down to the benefit of the GOP? Very simply, when people are in stress, they will eagerly seek help from anyone who tells them unequivocally that they have the TRUE ANSWER TO THE PROBLEMS WE'RE IN! Even if those ANSWERS are doubling down on the very creation of the PROBLEMS in the first place! It's easy to say, if they have no responsibility, that they "know how to create" bucko jobs! For the less informed, the difference between "knowing how & actually creating is seemingly the same!

However, for those critically trained, the difference is as GOOD as a mile in difference – <u>if the intent of the GOP is to maintain the status quo and not really do anything to fix the problem they created</u>! Why, you say? If you as the owners of huge businesses have now created the <u>next third world level working class</u>, do you think they would want to destroy it by giving people jobs leading to wage increases? You bet your Ass they don't! Keeping people poor, desperate, anxious, fearful is the <u>fundamental AIM of the (Greed Over People) party</u> to control the populous! With fear, they can suggest anything or blame anyone and <u>can count on having the desired result and response in their favor with a 90% degree of certainty</u>! They are the masters of marketing, branding and focus group studies!

As consumers of the propaganda you receive from the GOP, you have to ask the <u>SUBTERFUSE BUSTING</u> questions! <u>Who do they associate with, where do they get their funding, who do they seem to favor in legislation</u>? When the <u>answers are only the 1% and businesses</u> that have <u>never done you any favors</u>, like banks, wall street, huge energy companies, insurance companies, you have to bite the bullet and say, <u>none of these entities have my best interests at heart so these are not people I want to support nor ones I feel would support the middle class at all</u>! In fact, if you look at all the GOP candidates in the present times we live, <u>NONE OF THEM SUGGEST THAT THEY ARE FOR YOUR BEST INTERESTS</u> – except the propaganda they promote to fool you into voting for them! Now knowing the long term strategies of the Greed Over People's agenda to take over this country for a very long time, <u>YOU MUST NEVER EVER VOTE FOR GOP EVER AGAIN!</u>

CHAPTER 08

LACK OF SPENDABLE MONEY

Hey, hey, hey, this is a huge one! Perhaps you don't remember when Clinton took office after Bush#1 crashed the country into one of the GOP's favorite things to do, a huge GoP created depression & did it again last decade!

It's interesting why anyone would deliberately create a depression rather than do things to benefit the economy! They didn't just create a total depression, they created at the same time a HUGE DEFICIT! One is bad enough, but the combination is a really deadly powerful combination! What this means is they extracted all of the easily obtainable money from the MIDDLE CLASS and gave it to the 1%ers. At the same time they also bankrupted the government so that it had a HUGE DEFICIT! This allowed them to use the HUGE DEFICIT as a giant club to beat up America, WE THE PEOPLE, 99%ers into doing exactly what they wanted them to do – a very real form of BLACKMAIL!

You don't think this part of TRAP? Look at the budget crisis of last summer! Look at the hammer used to extend the Bush tax cuts for another year! Look at the Debt ceiling battle the Tea Baggers caused to down grade the United States credit rating for the first time in history! Perfect Trap!

Now, the PERFECT PART of the PERFECT TRAP! With We The People totally devoid of discretionary funds, they no longer have any CLOUT to fund campaigns against the GOP and corp. interests! Citizens United nailed the lid on that coffin – making the middle class totally IMPOTENT to compete with the huge corp/1%ers money! Perfect TRAP!

CHAPTER 09   19

NO MEANINGFUL RESPONSE TO NEEDS OF WE T PPL

With America losing jobs caused by the ReCorpiCONs at a hemorrhaging rate of over 800,000 jobs a month since 2007 and a total job loss being over 8 million jobs before Obama was even elected, you've created the most DIRE set of consequences for the new president & congress in 2009 and beyond. If there is a better set up for a PERFECT TRAP we've never seen it! Not only does Obama have to respond to a particularly bad economy, he has to also somehow create a HUGE number of jobs in a very short time with a totally hostile economy! With ReCorpiCONs swearing that government has absolutely no role in creating jobs, you have a force in the government that ideologically opposes any real attempt to change the jobless situation for the better! With McConnell pledging from the beginning that his # 1 job is making Obama a one term president, you have a totally hostile congress pledged to keep Obama from being successful at every thing that he might try to better the economy & create jobs in the USA! What a perfect set up for a Perfect TRAP!!

What is extraordinarily different about this depression, as opposed to ones prior to this one, is a condition - a large part of the GOP plan - that the ReCorpiCONs do not want to talk about AT ALL! Over at least the past decade they passed laws making it favorable to ship jobs over seas or to outsource American jobs to India, Pakistan, China or other Asian countries! Oddly enough, one of the most vocal proponents of this disastrous trend was the (BAIN OF YOUR LIVES) THAT ACTUALLY ADVERTISED THAT THEY

WERE PIONEER FACILITATORS OF THIS TREND. So unlike the past depressions where companies pared back to skeleton crews so they could expand when things got better, in this case, entire plants were closed and there was no way to come back and expand when things got better! <u>Jobs were just gone</u>! That <u>created a PERMANENT FORM OF REAL UNEMPLOYMENT</u> like no one had ever experienced before! This set up a ReCorpiCON mantra of "where's the beef" (Jobs)? <u>Well isn't that just convenient</u>?

Despite this dire background, <u>Obama was incredibly successful in first, stopping the hemorrhaging and then creating more than 4.6 million jobs in this hostile environment</u>! The ReCorpiCONs conveniently continue to use the Unemployment index as the measure of how well things are going rather than use the more meaningful bikini chart of job losses under the GOP versus the job creation under the Obama administration. You see, the Index will always be a near constant of over 8% even if you are creating jobs at 200,000 jobs a month! The new hires coming on the roles will always balance that until things get a Hell of a lot better economically! Keep in mind that had Obama not done anything that worked, the ReCorpiCON's favorite Unemployment index would have been well over 25% as the direct result of their OUTSOURCING & SHIPPING JOBS TO FOREIGN COUNTRIES. <u>The ReCorpiCON party of NO</u> has been <u>very successful at blocking every move to create jobs</u>! THEY CLEARLY PUT POLITICAL AGENDA BEFORE AMERICAs NEEDS OF GETTING OVER THIS ReCorpiCON CAUSED DIRE DEPRESSION. Since they have controlled the House, <u>THEY HAVE PASSED ZERO JOBS BILLS and passed over 29 vagina controlling bills</u>!

CHAPTER 10

LOSS OF RESPECT FOR PUBLIC SERVANTS

One of the <u>meanest parts</u> of the <u>PERFECT TRAP</u> waged by the Huge Propaganda Wars the ReCorpiCONs have been waging against America is the deliberate degradation of Public Servants, Professions and UNIONS. Looking at Wisconsin for example, one of the first things the new governor did to "fix the budget" was to go after the public Sector and their UNIONS. They vilified the school teachers, police and public healthcare professionals to justify cutting their benefits and wages <u>while reducing the number of them on the roles</u>. Keep in mind that the <u>state shortfall was deliberately created by the ReCorpiCONs in the past decade NOT THE UNIONS</u> – <u>so having built the problem</u>, they now use it to "fashion" a "solution" <u>to fix the problem that they Deliberately Created</u>. This is so patently obvious that even the very dummied down American should be able to figure it out – but they do not seem to get it! <u>They cheer when Public Servants are fired!</u>

This kind of propagandist abuse leaves the public with a <u>foul taste for public employees</u> and <u>thus by association all of government itself</u>! Have you not stopped to ask why the ReCorpiCON party <u>wants the public to despise Public Service and Public Service employees</u>? No brainer, no. 1 <u>they want to privatize everything that used to be public</u>! This allows the rich to own what had been public works and public based services so that they can <u>"live off of"</u> the "PUBLIC TROUGH" and at <u>Public expense</u>! <u>Guess who will be all for raising your taxes</u> when private corps own all of what used to be public works! <u>The ReCorpiCONS</u>!!!

22   Whatever it cost before, it's <u>going to cost at least 30% more when privatized!</u> <u>You MUST be warned of this TRAP!</u> What is more, privatization of public works leads to fraud, corruption, <u>definite lack of response to public needs based upon a profit motive and GREED!</u> A library will <u>no longer buy any books</u> because that cuts into the bottom line! Fire engine crews won't put out a fire at your house if you haven't paid the <u>"appropriation fee" in advance</u>"! Crews with busses won't go to pick up stranded people in a Katrina like disaster because moving the busses cuts into the bottom line <u>and abuses the GREED of the owners</u>! Public schools that have been made private will only spend the minimum of what they can to GET BY! Guess who losses! The ReCorpiCONs? Guess again, IT'S YOU<u>, IT'S YOU</u>! Oh yes, if you Privatize Jails, you will soon have kick backs, fraud and collusion with judges and jailers <u>to maximize occupancy at the public expense</u> – in all ways that you can imagine that can be accomplished! Are you the winners in this <u>new Public good</u>? <u>You know that you are not</u>! Only those who own public entities and are paid by public taxes <u>by people who will see to it your taxes will be raised again and again will be the winners</u>!

There is a definite reason that the "Common Good" can only BEST be served by a government entity <u>dedicated to service or the "common good"</u> rather than profit motive! That is why they were set up that way, why they have served so well for centuries & why privatization is a Grand mistake! <u>This ReCorpiCON wave to privatize everything is the latest attempt to grab the last public monies left to be GRABBED</u>! Pure Greed Over People) a continuation of the money grab of the past DECADE! <u>Did that work for you</u>?!

So where are we? ReCorpiCONs have successfully denigrated the image of public employees, and thus the image of governments of any kind, even more so the Federal Government! <u>This was the GOP DECADE goal!</u> Why do you think they generate so much propaganda about <u>HOW INEFFICIENT THE FED GOVERNMENT IS, HOW WASTEFUL IT IS, HOW MUCH BETTER CORPS COULD DO THE JOB, HOW MUCH BETTER PRIVATE SCHOOLS ARE, HOW MUCH GOVN SPENDS FOR A TOILET SEAT, HOW INEPT THE PUBLIC EMPLOYEES ARE, HOW LAZY THEY ARE AT THE JOB!</u> Do you think they spend 100's of millions on "Selling You" this concept for the <u>FUN of IT</u> or to spend money as a loss leader? No, <u>they are deadly serious about "selling you" TOTAL LIES to serve their purpose of taking over YOUR MIND & RENDERING IT USELESS TO DISTINGUISH What is real and what is TOTALLY FALSE TO CONTROL YOUR VOTE!!</u>

You've got to STOP being influenced by this propaganda! You <u>must get to critically thinking about what you hear, rather than reacting to it emotionally</u> – which is exactly what they want you to do! <u>Keep in mind the GOP are the masters</u> of FOCUS GROUPS, BRANDING AND MARKETING PHRASES TO <u>CONVINCE PEOPLE TO BUY</u> WHAT <u>NORMALLY THEY WOULD CONSIDER TO BE PURE BULL SHIT & CRAPOLA!</u>

More seriously, the No. 2 goal of the GOP is to either not pay anything for our governments or otherwise starve it to death or BOTH. Their goal is to take the taxes for the rich to ZERO and starting at 90% in the 50-60's they are to 35% (14% for Romney) now or <u>60% of the way there now!</u> Romney wants it to be 20% for the rich. <u>DO YOU NOT GET IT? DO YOU NOT SEE WHO is BEING SCREWED BY the GOP? You've got to stop this by NEVER Voting GOP ever again!!</u>

SUMMARY OF WHAT WE'VE LEARNED

With the multiple, radial causes leading to the PERFECT TRAP being effective in creating the conditions that will totally ensnare <u>VOTERS into thinking that the VERY SAME GOP THAT CREATED THE TRAP WILL BE THE ONES THAT ARE BEST SUITED TO GET THEM OUT OF THE TRAP</u>, we have a black widow waiting at the center to ensure that WE THE PEOPLE will never get out of the trap <u>Unless you get smart!</u>

Let's review the radial causes leading into the PERFECT TRAP! These are: Two unpaid for wars; One unpaid for Medicare part D; taking a $5 trillion Democratically created surplus into a $10.7 trillion GOP created deficit; Unregulated Over the Counter derivatives that crashed the housing markets and economies; Hubris, lack of transparency and Obfuscation of purposes; $3 trillion tax cut for the rich; Total deregulation of Energy, financial & insurance companies; greed & rip offs of We The People!

These are the GOP planned & generated conditions that set up the PERFECT TRAP! The ten circular rungs described in chaps 1 through 10 are the ensnaring "silks" that catch & hold the unwary Democrats and Independent voters in the PERFECT TRAP so that the Greed Over People <u>(GOP) party can devour their bodies and bones for all time.</u> <u>(Money, salary, retirements, savings, political clout)</u> The very image, the PERFECT TRAP & spider, should instill fear by itself but <u>knowing the details of how long this TRAP has been planned</u> and set in motion <u>should put a total Shudder up your Spine and Freeze Your Blood</u>. YOU MUST ALL BY THIS PARABLE GET TO <u>KNOW WHO AND WHAT YOU ARE DEALING WITH & JUST VOTE THE GOP BASTARDS OUT</u>!!

Having lived in Delaware when you were first elected to the Senate, <u>you will know of what I speak</u> when I talk about the DuPont estate above the Brandywine and the gun powder works below on the river. **THIS IS SO IMPORTANT TO YOU AND Barack's CAMPAIGN THAT I CANNOT OVER STRESS THE POINT!** DuPont was <u>educated in chemistry</u> (and other sciences, perhaps) in France under Lavoisier. Being well to do, he moved to Delaware and built a lovely home above the Brandywine. The story is vague, but as I recall, the young American Army came to him and asked if he would use his <u>scientific knowledge</u> to supply gun powder to the army efforts. He built the powder works JUST BELOW HIS HOME IN ACCORD WITH HIS PERSONAL BELIEF THAT WHEN YOU START A COMPANY OF THIS KIND, THE <u>OWNER SHARES THE RISK WITH THE WORKERS & THE PLANT</u>. The plant was built with numerous safety features and was close enough to where he lived for <u>him to become directly involved in a tragedy if it occurred</u>. <u>He shared the risk</u> with his workers!

Why is this so important then and so extremely important now? It is very simple, it was the very basis of how this great nation was built – <u>mutual trust</u>, <u>shared risk</u>, science, technology, innovation and an always meaningful active eye on safety <u>and the well being of the workers who might be at great risk</u>! There is no question that he had the BIG house and made the lions' share of the money but he built that plant & almost every plant since in more than 100 years of DuPont on the foundation of safety first, technologies, and shared risk. There wasn't a month go by that we did not have safety inspections even in the safe areas of the labs and took great pride in having totally accident free years. They safely built technical products for over a century!! Far cry from a Bain Capital!

The second point is, all of DuPont to this day is based upon development of products and services based upon science and technology of some kind! A fact that the ReCorpiCONs either don't know or choose to ignore, appreciate or rally around. You do not make a scientist, engineer, technologist or any other productive person in development in a few days, months or a year. You do not make great scientists in a 4 hr/night school or on-line learning! You do not become a Principal Scientist just by having a "buddy" put a title behind your name like the ReCorpiCONs seem to think you can do. It takes decades starting from grade school to train productive people! This is a fact that many of those ReCorpiCONs who, with little training themselves recently built fortunes on the demise of the real people's jobs and now seem to forget or simply just do not care! Tektronix, Hewlett Packard, GE, Sylvania, Westinghouse, Magnavox, TI, Ford, GM, Micro Soft, Intel, Apple, Google, all of the Military Industrial complex companies in the 50's – 60's in Silicon Valley and Rt 128 around Boston, SRI and on and on, were based on and centered around areas of great research and education such as Stanford, Cal, MIT, Carnegie Mellon, the science triangle in the SE. The once proud Interstate highway systems that <u>the rich and big companies all benefited from immensely</u> have fallen into decay. The heyday of this country in products and development, and achieving the American Dream was in the 50's – 60's when the highest tax rate was well over 90%. When you started a company then, the idea came first and you <u>built the company to stay and grow for a very long time</u> –not like now where the ReCorpiCON dream is to rip everyone off & make a quick BUCK. <u>What was</u> the American Dream should be once again! What is needed is a great DEMOCRAT Commitment!

I remember a 50's cartoon in the New Yorker picturing a college campus at graduation where a Student in mortar board and gown was hog tied to a pole and being carried off by two "suits" and the caption of two bystanders read, "Well, I see DuPont got another one". That was the climate! The co's from all over America clamored to be able to go to these campuses and recruit the top new scientists and business students actively and aggressively. If you didn't have interview trips to at least 6 great companies, you were a piker or an idiot. Where are the ads that fill 6-10 full pages of the Sunday papers? Perhaps gone to Asia, India, China, Pakistan, Korea. We can all thank the ReCorpiCONs agenda for this. They see their markets in those parts of the world and seemingly do not care if America even exists at all – except, perhaps, as a really cheap third world type labor! That is not the American Dream and it never was the American Dream and if the Democrats can make that point repeatedly and consistently, it need not become and continue to be "their American Dream"! Just make it BOLD & Memorable & strike a blow for American workers, and the hopefully soon rejuvenation of the upwardly bound Middle Class! <u>Keep in mind, the</u>

28   <u>ReCorpiCONs hate a strong middle class, because they are too educated, too mobile and have too much money and CAN THINK FOR THEMSELVES, have influence and can steer elections for the good of WE THE PEOPLE</u>. The ReCorpiCONs need total ignorance and blind acceptance of what they are "taught" to succeed! They need a truly dummied down America to win!

So, are the ReCorpiCONs, really interested in returning this country to true greatness and strength in the world markets or are they just doing lip service to the "Jobs effort" <u>that was responsible for the 8 million job loss in 2007-08</u> Keep in mind, that tax cuts have <u>never created</u> one job, nor will it ever create one job. Try building a bridge with Tax Cuts, Try building public highways, power plants, jails, schools with tax cuts. That is not to mean that huge tax increases beyond a reasonable ability to pay will improve the economy either. When business is taxed in a meaningful way for the <u>privilege of being able to create wealth as a result of the extreme benefit</u>s provided to them by common governmental efforts – access to valuable resources like Oil, minerals, public lands, public timber, working rail systems, advanced, effective highway systems, internet, mail, libraries, telecommunications, radio/tv to name a few and they are allowed to flourish enormously as the result of people trained by public universities and other government aided sources of talent – <u>why should they not be expected to pay back</u> a very large reasonable amount to that government for being able to use those publicly provided benefits/privileges. Many of them pay nothing, ZERO, nada, ZIP!! Look what the Military/NASA monies did to stimulate new products and new technological areas for development into products and businesses! They forget that they did not get to their greatness and wealth <u>on only their own efforts</u> without the extreme benefit of valuable resources provided for them at a modest cost that made them able to achieve far more than their foreign competitors. <u>Now foreign competitors are using these benefits to over take us</u>!

In-coming foods, do not inspect themselves, nor police what has been applied to them in foreign countries. Imported products do not police themselves as to inferior, destructive or poisonous materials!! The Libertarians want to take us back to an Agrarian society when we grew our own foods and knew, more or less, what we did to them or put on them! In present global markets, who in hell knows who pissed or shit on the vegetables or berries that come into the United States. Who in hell knows what terrible pesticides were sprayed on our foods before they get here! By loosing direct control of what we eat and use, we need to replace that loss with something effective to keep us all safe. That requires a strong government, government regulations and government inspectors and that costs <u>everyone</u> some money. <u>These people apparently do not know the origin of the concept of insurance</u>. It started, ironically, in a very global and capitalistic setting!

In the early days of merchant ships that went out on the seas to foreign countries to buy and sell goods, things being what they were, there were losses of ships and goods in storms, by pirates and other disasters. People had put up good money to invest in a ship, crew and goods to make money only to have a net loss if the ship is lost or never returns. In taverns by the docks, people put up signup boards to put down money to take a risk on ships, or crews. These "contracts" grew because more often than not the ship's trips were successful and everyone made out like bandits. Perhaps, a ship was lost, and as a result the owner of the ship was not at a total loss, because of this common money pool that in effect covered that one loss, while benefiting from all of the other successes. Lloyds' of London was purported to start this way. <u>Soc S is a form of insurance so we don't all lose</u>.

<u>So, the common good became the norm to trump truly private and independent efforts to do business</u>. You would not live in a $500,000 house without fire, theft, etc. insurance. You shouldn't drive a car without casualty and liability insurance. Why, because, a small accident could cause your financial ruin for the rest of your life. <u>Shared risk and shared benefits</u>. That is what a government is and does <u>for not only people, but free enterprise and businesses</u>. But it has to be set up by law and run, more or less, by the government that enacted it as well as being paid for to be effective. <u>Common benefits are not free</u>, but the alternatives are a total disaster and if <u>enough of them prevail</u>, <u>have real consequences for the entire nation and commerce as a whole</u>. See Katrina, Haiti, BP negligence caused Oil disaster in the Gulf. No one local government, state or regional government can deal effectively with these and like disasters. <u>It takes the common good to make a real difference</u>.

Back to DuPont and its significant consequences. 31
I am not against corps, you are not against corps, and Democrats are not against corps! That is fact Number 1 that should be broadcast to the entire country. A company like DuPont was constantly involved in trying to develop useful products that served real needs and met those needs at the lowest cost with the highest level of performance available at the cost. As a result, people had jobs and made good money to enjoy the good life and American Dream while giving them a possible path to <u>better times and perhaps starting companies of their own</u>. All good, and all happened until about 2000. Tektronix, HP were always on top of competing with each other to better serve the needs of their customers. That kind of competition is good! <u>However, corps that do nothing but take money from us to make more money for themselves and a few top brass at our expense should be severely taxed, or put out of business</u>.

These companies are not a DuPont, Tektronix or HP etc. These are vultures and produce NOTHING OF VALUE FOR THE COMMON GOOD! When a corporation exists only for the reason of taking good companies in trouble and using the assets to take out huge loans that are ripped off by the acquiring company leaving the company to falter under the debt and die – that is not free enterprise, nor productive to produce the American Dream. When a company <u>bets on the decimation and destruction of a business</u> and wins royally when that demise occurs – <u>that is not free enterprise nor the spirit that built these United States nor the American Dream. Yes, Bah Humbug!</u>

32   So where is DuPont now? It's still there & so are the two spin-offs that reside near DuPont in Delaware. This is the image that you should be projecting when you talk & campaign. This is the future that you should be projecting for America! This is the message that has to be brought to light when you campaign. Now, if you just happen to point out along the way, the many ways that the <u>ReCorpiCONs have destroyed that American Dream & image, you can't be faulted for your honest perspective of the facts. You are the messenger, not the purveyor</u>!

Some other ideas. Since the ReCorpiCONs seem to be against anything that you do, or that will help your image (Clearly if they are so paranoid of your winning, <u>they must really fear how truly effective you are at countering their agenda and propaganda</u>) take matters into your own hands. Is there not TARP money left over? Use that money to set up "venture" capital to start truly high tech, high paying and high yield companies. This is similar to what Clinton did by using (then) $50million through DARPA to stimulate established companies like Tektronix, TI, Sarnoff etc. to develop the then fledgling flat panel display technologies so that they would not all go to Asia. This program was extremely successful and was used to start some small companies as well. DARPA being military is directly under your direction as Commander in Chief. Pick new technologies important to the military as well as the economy and spend away without Congressional approval. This could be a PR winner as well the same way Kennedy's we're going to the moon was then. Use it very effectively. There are plenty of the right scientists, technologists and managers around to set these companies up fast and make them effective. YOU MUST USE EVERY OPPORTUNITY!

Use charts and graphs effectively to show progress & RIGHT DIRECTION! We must restore the AMERICAN DREAM – MAKE THAT THE CENTER PIECE OF YOUR MESSAGE IN STATE OF UNION & ON TOUR! You will win – thus we will all win. <u>The alternative is UNCONSCIONABLE</u>!

Now that the ReCorpiCON primaries are in full swing, I feel that you need to be reminded of the big picture – <u>the why of the why</u> – the real agenda that you will eventually have to fight very effectively before September through November this year. <u>You must not be fooled by their well planned schemes and propagandas</u>!

Obviously, the ReCorpiCONs want this election to be about two things: 1. a total "hate definition" of a "totally incompetent", "do nothing" Obama and the "so called" Obama administration directed totally toward the destruction of America; and 2. to obfuscate the true issues by making it an <u>election</u> about a personality, an individual, a face, a <u>glad hand</u>, a "philosophy" of one candidate that would be running against you! They ignore the irony that for a party that totally hates the big bad government to do anything but get smaller, they should be "praising" Obama for DOING SO LITTLE rather than blaming him for doing nothing! THIS IS PURE BULL SHIT! <u>They simply cannot have it both ways! They say that Govn cannot create jobs yet promise they will create 12 million jobs in the first four years of GOP admin</u>!

34   It doesn't matter if the selected candidate is the "normally" moderate, now "turned Conservative" flip flopping Rommley; or the for a decade predictable Ron Paul; the totally loose cannon, Gingrinch; the totally unrealistically polished, smiling Christian evangelistically faced – "Wal-mart manager", Sanitorium, or the almost reasonably spoken and apparently thoughtful, though low on the totem pole, Huntsman. Forget, Perry, he burned his bridges so long ago, that there is no real prospect for him to make it. THANK GOD FOR THAT!! The last thing this country needs is an even more ignorant, ideological GW Shrub!

The amazing thing that is now apparent to most of the world, (though perhaps not most of America) is that these 7-8 totally ignorant idiots would actually get on a national (world wide) stage, not once but many times, and shout to the world that they are TOTALLY IGNORANT IDIOTS! Not only would they shout this absurdity to the world but THEY'RE <u>DAMNED</u> PROUD of it! Oh, I forgot, they are ReCorpiCON IDIOTS SO THEY REALLY DO NOT KNOW ANY BETTER. THEY WERE PERHAPS HOME SCHOOLED! I have digressed so I will get back to the point!

THE POINT IS THIS: DO NOT BE FOOLED BY THIS, NEITHER YOU NOR YOUR ADVISORY TEAM BE FOOLED BY THIS CHARADE, THIS TOTAL DIVERSION FROM WHAT SHOULD BE YOUR ONLY ISSUE AND FOCUS IN THIS ELECTION. YOU HAVE STARTED IN THE RIGHT DIRECTION, SO DO NOT BE DIVERTED FROM THE COURSE!

<u>*IT DOES NOT MATTER WHO THE CANDIDATE IS*</u> ON THE OTHER SIDE, <u>THEY ARE ALL ReCorpiCONS</u> AND HAVE BUT

ONE AGENDA & THAT IS THE ReCorpiCON agenda as it's been since Reagan! Support the rich and corps. at all expense. Shrink taxes for rich & corps to zero and shrink government (social services, SS, Medicare) to zero.

Your focus has to be against the ReCorpiCON agenda, regardless of who the candidate turns out to be – BECAUSE IT TRULY DOESN'T MATTER WHO IT IS, THEY WILL STILL BE ReCorpiCONs and will push the GOP agenda!!

See addictinginfo.org if it's still there for a complete list of ReCorpiCON goals for America. See Alecexposed.com and other sites for full disclosure of ReCorpiCON agenda and goals) After 2010 they have foolishly made those agendas and goals very clear by the actions in the House, Tea Party ReCorpiCONs, Koch brother controlled State houses in Wisconsin, Mich, Fla, Ind, Pa etc.. They have spilled their guts for the world to see and evaluate!

No. 1 agenda is to bankrupt the government in a way to cause either by implied reason to curtail or the actual curtailment by strangulation of funds - what has been till now very successful "liberal" programs like SS, medicare and Medicaid. No. 2, they want to reduce or totally eliminate all regulations of business while at the same time regulating all other People of These United States to the hilt! That makes two distinct classes of American Citizens (thanks to Citizens United and the biased, legislation from the bench -Supreme Court) which is clearly unconstitutional! There cannot be two distinctly different classes of people to be treated in distinctly different ways under the law where Federal law is concerned. Run that one by these so called

36   Constitutional Conservatives and see how it grinds a Ron Paul!

<u>Bankrupting America as a means to a "greater" end is not only very effective</u> it is so transparent that the "ingrained propagandized" America is apparently incapable of recognizing it. <u>They think that it is just a terrible thing that just happened to them and now they're encouraged to blame Obama for it</u>. They have to be severely "educated" on this subject and <u>constantly reminded</u> that America being in this present state <u>was no accident,</u> nor an unintended consequence of a few bad apples in the barrel! You might well ask, why would they want to do that if a ReCorpiCON candidate like McCain might have been elected? Simple, it makes it even easier if the man at the top and the congress are sympathetic to the <u>end goals</u> and will use that bankruptcy fact to speed legislation to further bankrupt America and the middle class that used to be the mainstay of America. It greases the wheels to their ends so much faster and easier! Look at how those "means" are being used so effectively in Wis., Fla., Ind., Mich., Pa. etc. to totally redefine the roll of governments, <u>the rights of voters</u>, and the <u>privatization of "public"</u> entities like schools, libraries, jails, municipalities, dams power plants, utilities, police depts., etc.

The end result, is two fold, the public gets to fund on a demand basis, private entities and have the public bail them out when they fail – <u>even though the funds all go to private investors</u>. And you think taxes will not be <u>suddenly raised a lot</u> when these "once public, private entities" suddenly need a lot more money to run? Do you think that <u>judges will not be on the take</u> to fill those jails to capacity? Do you think that if it costs X dollars to run a public run county jail that it will not cost at least X+30% to run the same privately run county jail? Do you think that public libraries will ever buy another book if it is run by a BOTTOM LINE DRIVEN private firm? Think again!!

And schools, (I could just kill Ron Wyden) do you think that middle city kids will ever get an education when schools go private, or that there are public "vouchers" to let the rich go to private schools? This serves only the rich and eventually the <u>"public" schools will no longer be funded</u> and will disappear and thus the lower middle and lower classes will just be SOL! No, this is not Democracy, nor the Democracy of our founding fathers! A <u>universal public education</u> was the <u>Foundation of the founding of America</u> and for a very good reason. They knew and had experienced what happened in England with so called "public" and private schools in England They believed that a universally educated and informed American public was the only way to make a true Democracy work. What kind of democracy do we now have with "so called" <u>home schooling</u> where <u>propaganda</u> can be taught, young minds poisoned by <u>anti-scientific bogus theories</u>, myths, and dogma in the guise of "public education"? We're reaping the dire consequences of this Ignorant Nonsense in the House of Reps and the present ReCorpiCON politics and presidential candidates. You only have to listen to Michael Bachmann for two minutes to figure that out! <u>Privatization</u> of public responsive entities is a <u>sure road to total ruin, corruption, bribery, scandal, shenanigans and</u>

38   <u>all forms of criminal corruption</u>. New Orleans lost its shipping trade because too many "hands were out" and on the take! JUST BAD FOR AMERICA. JUST BAD FOR ANY COUNTRY OR ENTITY! Just bad for the Middle Class!

Now for the second scene: The ReCorpiCON created bankrupt economy gives a purpose to cutting badly needed necessary services for the children, poor, elderly, sick, infirm, homeless, jobless and mentally ill segments of our population at the local, state & national levels. Senior citizens are being <u>made to pay for things</u> they could not afford at any time, but especially now when their retirements have been systematically and severely attacked and reduced by so many ReCorpiCON means that they are too numerous to count here. Because of retirement or devastating situations, those least able to cope with cost increases are being asked to take on the resulting burden of a national debt and economic crisis that was created by the rich 1% ReCorpiCONs who not only escaped punishment for their grossly corrupt inappropriate acts but instead were rewarded for them by being bailed out by the poor, and elderly's dimes and nickels and adding injury to insult, <u>were then treated to bonuses and salary increases while Rome burned</u>!

One other significant point, Never ever call SS, medicare, Medicaid an <u>entitlement program ever again</u>! It is an "insurance policy" paid into by the participants over their lifetime of work and as such is a firm commitment to be paid when eligible. If run like an insurance company, it would be actuarially funded forever to be solvent to make its payments. <u>Perhaps to appease the Corporatists,</u>

<u>you'd propose that the received funds be managed by 10 top investment funds to make as much money in bad times as well as good on the premiums that have been collected to pay for the "insurance" or annuity.</u> Those firms would be selected every two years based upon their last ten years of performance so that no one firm is ever assured a lifetime "take" on the public monies. Their fees will be totally regulated by Fed Government law for this "opportunity" to make money off of the public funds provided to them. This would shut up the ReCorpiCON argument that these funds should be handled by private investments. After all, one of the top ReCorpiCON agendas is to get private hands on all of the remaining public monies available to RIP OFF! This way it works for America as well as Wall Street. It is a true WIN WIN FOR ALL OF US!! This alone could surely make you a winner in 2012!

Note to President Obama: 2/3/12

One of the most powerful NEGATIVE words in the English language is the word NO! NO is the weakest willed and safest words one can use to obstruct progress! Using NO is very unique in several ways. If something of value is proposed and stopped with the vote of NO, you can almost never prove that decision wrong! You see, when you stop something of greatness with a NO vote it doesn't get done and therefore, the outcome or benefit can never be measured or demonstrated. You as the proposer can never be allowed to make the point effectively of how much value it produced or you provided by implementing it. It's back to entropy! Nature on it's own votes NO and therefore any idiot can vote NO and expend no energy and never suffer consequences. On the other hand it takes real courage, risk, global view, stick-too-it-iv-ness, compass, morals, stamina, fortitude, value, guts, future thinking to vote YES! It takes real effort, commitment, vision to see a brighter future and much work against huge odds and mighty destructive forces to take a NO to a YES! Saying yes to progress is GODs work!

Therefore, those who vote YES to the future should be applauded, rewarded, commended, celebrated and encouraged for they have done much work and taken on risk for the future. On the contrary, those who vote NO to the future must be ridiculed, ignored, condemned, diminished, minimalized, punished, decried or shunned because they have not just ACCOMPLISHED PRECISELY NOTHING – THEY HAVE GONE BEYOND AND PREVENTED OUR VERY FUTURE! THEY HAVE HANDED OUR COMPETITIVENESS, GREATNESS, NATIONAL HONOR OVER to our COMPETITOR'S COUNTRIES! They are beneath our contempt - not worth the time of day, or the time or money to pay their keep! They are the true lechers and <u>therefore are the domestic terrorists to our very lives</u>! To pay them a wage is <u>like paying for a goof off, a total loafer, dead beat, a do nothing and must stop ASAP</u>!

You need to continually ask these questions of your crowds; "<u>How many companies do you know that were started on a vote of NO</u>?" How many companies were grown to greatness with a vote of NO? <u>How many "jobs" were created along the way or by these companies with a NO as a basis</u>? How many of our great (in the 50's – 60's) interstate highways were started and built with a vote of NO? <u>Risk nothing and gain nothing and LOSE</u>! <u>It takes money to make money</u> – a resounding Republican Truth. Starting a company takes a lot of up front money and a long time before it even breaks even – a fact well known by ReCorpiCONs as well as everyone else!

Getting to greatness in something like infrastructure, a race to the moon, conquering outer space, getting the economy back, getting companies to hire, etc. takes horrendous amounts of money up front to even be able to have a chance at making the journey in the future. However, the benefits to industry, products, technologies, general science, <u>stimulus to education are horrendous & the return on investment are 100's to 1000's of times over</u>. A prime example is the landing on Mars and its benefits!

Most people fail to realize that <u>All OF THESE 1% ers BENEFITED THE MOST FROM ALL OF THESE PROGRAMS</u> -- GREAT PUBLIC UNIVERSITIES, LIBRARIES, NASA, ELECTRICAL

42 GRIDS, SUPER HIGHWAYS, RAILROADS, FREE LEASES OF OIL FIELDS, INTERNET, TELEVISION, RADIO AND SATALITES. THIS GREATNESS DIDN'T JUST START IN A VACUUM, OR OVER NIGHT - IT WAS BUILT BY OUR GOVERNMENTS DURING AMERICA'S HEYDAY IN THE '50s – '60s WHEN TOP TAXES WERE OVER 90%. <u>YES, THE 1%ers BENEFITED THE MOST FROM THESE GOVERN FUNDED PROGRAMS WHILE THEY ENJOYED THE AMERICAN DREAM!</u> HAVING MADE GREAT FORTUNES AS THE RESULT OF THESE ADVANTAGES THAT AMERICA FUNDED FOR THEM THEY <u>SEEM TO FEEL THE TIME FOR ANYONE ELSE BENEFITING IS OVER!! THEY HAVE BEEN STRANGLING THIS GREATNESS SINCE REAGAN BY SHRINKING THE REVENUE (TAXES 50% OR HIGHER) AND SQUANDERING IT TO THE REST OF THE WORLD!</u> WHY? BECAUSE THEY <u>ARE REFUSING TO FUND GREATNESS AND INSTEAD ARE OPTING FOR MEDIOCRITY!   THEY NEED TO SAY YES TO GREATNESS, THE FUTURE AND YES TO GROWTH AND PROSPERITY NOW!</u> <u>Don't just say NO to the future!</u>

PEOPLE ARE FOOLED BY THIS ReCorpiCON PROPAGANDA AND AGENDA INTO THINKING THAT 1. REDUCING TAXES WILL STIMULATE THE ECONOMY – HISTORY CLEARLY SAYS OTHERWISE! 2. THAT REDUCING THE DEFICIT (AND JOBS & EMPLOYMENT) WILL RESTORE THE ECONOMY! It only increases UNEMPLOYMENT AND GIVES THEM A PROPAGANDA TOOL TO SHRINK THE GOVERNMENT EVEN MORE! THEY WANT TO CURTAIL, BY LACK OF FUNDING, THE SOCIAL PROGRAMS THAT HAVE SAVED THIS COUNTRY 100'S OF MILLIONS OF TIMES – ONE PERSON at a TIME! WELL, <u>THEY DESTROYED THIS COUNTRY NOW THEY HAVE TO PAY FOR THE DAMAGES BY INCREASES IN THEIR TAXES!</u>

Note to President Obama 2/29/12

If you ever end up debating Risky Sanitorium and he has just ended one of his Religious based dogma tirades, and it is your time to speak, you might just stand there looking at him in a sort of disbelief for several moments and then, looking at your watch briefly, slowly ask, "this is the 21st century is it not? Not the 20th or 19th Century, right?" Well, I have traveled the world in the past three years and to the best of my knowledge, I do not know of a single place in the modern world where your kind of politically religious thinking would be welcome. Yes, this is America where we have and believe in Religious Freedom and thinking. Because we are in America you are free to believe any way you want about <u>your own God or Religion</u> but for the very same reason, your Religious Thinking has absolutely no place in this or any other Form of a Democracy, politics or government and By GOD, it will not become any part of this great Nation's politics, government, governance or laws if I can do anything to prevent it! And just stop there and sit down. Even a 19th century America isn't ready for this kind of dogmatic simplicity!

Short sighted "principles" have real, often disastrous consequences that "simple" minded Dogma and "Simple" statements can neither comprehend nor anticipate. These real consequences are most often razor edged, extremely serious and non-reversibly detrimental on a widespread basis! That doesn't ever seem to bother a dogmatist in a dummied down society. <u>Compromise, the basis of a Democracy and this great government and Constitution</u> is simply not an option to a

44 dogmatist nor do they even consider it as a part of a process to get to the "absolute" goal that they seek. As a result, they become the very thing they hate everywhere else, <u>the American Taliban</u>! No place here for stupidity!

I'm sure you have noticed that all of a sudden when all the good news seems to be going your way, every "liberal" news cast blasts that the price of gas is going through the roof despite the fact that it went over $6.00 under Bush and no one seemed to notice a bit. Big deal, it has gone up and down many times under both Bush and now. It is the constant hottest item blasting that is so blatantly transparent and also helps the ReCorpiCON speculators run it up some more in time for the election. Next time you talk on the campaign trail you might take the tack: "If I had <u>one tenth</u> the magical powers that the ReCorpiCONs attribute to me for "running this country into the ground", do you think for a minute that I would use those "horrendous powers" to do real damage to this great country – especially in an election year? <u>It's crazy</u>!

If I had those terrible powers <u>that they continually attribute to me of being able to grossly affect gasoline prices</u>, <u>do you think I am so stupid as to use them to raise them to new heights in an election year</u>? Do you really think that anyone, particularly me, would use these horrendous powers to do real damage to this great country rather than trying desperately to try to counter the errors and damages that were left to me when I took office? No, we have accomplished a lot to turn this great country around in it's time of great need. The stock market's now over the magical number of 13,000 from 6,000 when I took office. We passed the most effective health care bill in over 60 years benefiting not just 35 million who were without, but all of the senior citizens as well as most of the rest of the people of these United States. We passed the most effective financial regulation and public protection law of the past 3 generations. We have turned around an 800,000/mo job loss before you were elected to an increase in private sector jobs of over 4.6 million with steady increases for almost all of those 36 months. This is in spite of the huge ReCorpiCON instigated public sector job losses. We have done a lot, but a lot more is needed to get us back to pre ReCorpiCON years. If you think that those who drove this great nation into this ditch of 2008 either know how to get it out <u>or much more importantly even want to get it out</u>? Can they be trusted to get it out? Remember, only the rich benefit from depressions/recessions, because they have the money to buy up everything at 10 cents on the dollar. We, on the other hand, don't even have money to eat or enjoy life during the same period of time without taking two jobs for both men and women and dipping into whatever savings/retirements we may have left after the GREAT ReCorpiCON raid on We The People during 2000-2008.

Do you think they're giving you negative press & spending $100's millions of dollars to get you out if they believe that you are the <u>most ineffective president of all time</u>? If you're so ineffective, why do they spend so much to get you out? The answer is they fear for what you will be able to do if you stay in office. Guess what, they cannot have it both ways. Either you are very effective at blocking their path to corporatism and fascism, or they really don't have any real plan that will

46   benefit WE THE PEOPLE of these united states so have to use subterfuge to make a case to keep us from being effective at regaining our stature we had under Clinton and before. How many people would you <u>respect</u> that buys a huge yacht and put it on your children & grandchildren's credit cards? Well, look who did that with glee and are now trying to blame that on you, and at the same time use that huge debt as a huge club to beat the 99% ers into believing that they have to sacrifice more to get that debt reduced. Simple math, when the rich pay less, to run this government, you have to pay a lot more. They ran it into th<u>e ditch so now they have to pay for the damage to the country and pay to get it out of the ditch!</u>

Note to President Obama 3/6/12

I heard your speech/press conference on the morning of Super Tuesday elections in Ohio, etc. I heard you use my comment: If I had those terrible powers <u>that they continually attribute to me of being able to grossly effect gasoline prices</u>, <u>do you think I am so stupid as to use them to raise them to new heights in an election year</u>?

However, you missed a terribly important comment and "definition" that you clearly should have made when you were asked about Dems claiming the ReCorpiCONs were against women and women's rights! (I realize it is hard to think on your feet in these situations) All you needed to point to is the following: Looking at the 2010 forward House of Reps, some 29 plus bills have been passed to restrict, regulate, control and minimalize women's vagina and women's rights. How many bills have been passed to create jobs - ZERO! How many were passed to increase the economy - ZERO! How much effort was expended to destroy this economy, good faith and excellent financial standing of these United States – several crucial, critical months of shenanigans did it!!

The answer, simply is, that it is not the Democrats who are making the case for ReCorpiCONs being against women – IT IS THE RcCorpiCONs THAT <u>ARE DEFINING THEMSELVES AS THOSE WHO ARE AGAINST</u> WOMEN'S RIGHTS AND ANTI WOMEN BY THEIR VERY STRIDENT ACTIONS in CONGRESS AND STATE HOUSES ACROSS THE country! It is not only the Democrat's right, but, YES, the extremely <u>IMPORTANT RESPONSIBILITY</u>, to POINT THIS OUT TO THE AMERICAN PUBLIC! <u>THIS, YOU SHOULD DO CONSTANTLY IN FUTURE</u>!

48 The same goes for their cries of Dems Starting a Class Warfare! It needs to be pointed out that the <u>real class warfare</u> was <u>started by ReCorpiCONs, over 30 years ago</u> by Reagan and others who stealthily, silently in the background & in obscure phrases in legislation since have WAGED CLASS WARFARE AGAINST THE MIDDLE CLASS AND ALL OF THE 99% ers as well. This is not a war started by DEMOCRATSs but DEMOCRATSs are using their <u>GOD given responsibilities to merely cast light</u> on what the ReCorpiCONs have been <u>waging on them for over a generation and are now nearly totally successful</u>!! Don't blame the Democrats for being the messenger! <u>It is their GOD given right</u> to <u>EXPOSE & ILLUMINATE this in order to make a DEMOCRACY VIABLE</u>!! We have GOD's right!

Note to President Obama 4/10/12

Great talk and in most cases you nailed it to them like a hand to the cross! However, you have to make it stick even harder than vague references. You need to spell it out that they have DELIBERATELY crept the tax code down for the rich from 72% under their HERO Reagan to 35% and want to get it to 25% <u>with DELIBERATELY vague promises of tax reform and loop hole closing</u>, but in fact have no real plans to do that or will not admit to what they will be. <u>They have already shown their true colors by voting down all previous attempts to close many of those loopholes.</u> As an example there are the Huge tax subsidies to energy companies. The 72% that was good enough for their dear idol Reagan should be good enough for them now! They are nickel and diming us down the path to <u>A BIG FAT ZERO with a no return policy ala Grover Norquist</u>. YOU HAVE GOT TO MAKE THE POINT OVER AND OVER AGAIN THAT <u>WHEN THE RICH 10% PAY LESS</u>, WE THE PEOPLE ARE THE ONES WHO <u>HAVE TO MAKE UP THE DIFFERENCE BY PAYING A LOT MORE</u> OR LOSE WHATEVER WE HAVE EARNED AND WORKED HARD TO ACQUIRE OVER THE PAST CENTURY! IT IS A <u>ZERO NET SUM GAME</u>! WHAT GOES OUT ONE PLACE HAS TO BE MADE UP SOMEWHERE ELSE WHICH SIMPLY MEANS WHEN THEIR TAXES GO DOWN, OURS, AS A CONSEQUENCE, ACTAULLY HAVE TO GO UP – A LOT! <u>THIS CANNOT BE SIMPLER TO STATE OR SIMPLER TO UNDERSTAND</u>! YOU HAVE GOT TO GET THAT MESSAGE TO THE 99% AND <u>ESPECIALLY TO THE LOWER INCOME BASE OF THE REPUBLICAN PARTY</u>!

<u>That is why this election is so critical!</u> We have to get the house and senate and state houses back to make this

50   really work for the middle class or all of our fates are sealed for a very long time. If they get a republican president in, <u>they will wrap up the supreme court for at least the next half century</u>! Hitler talked of the 1000yr Reich! Tying up state houses, House and Senate and Supreme Court with voter suppression/gerrymandering is one large way to achieve that sort of thing. We'll be and Y'All be "<u>DAMNED</u>" ala TA HAUSROUND. The <u>Republican primary is nothing more than a huge DIVERSION to keep America's eyes off what they have planned for state houses, governorships and the house and senate races</u>!!! That is their goal and real agenda to take over the very lives of every American's future! <u>They falsely talk about less government giving personal freedom. They want nothing less than to take away all your freedoms and increase government while losing regulations for corps.</u>!

Again, point out that if you had the enormous power over the oil prices that they attribute to you in a negative sense, you would never raise them – especially in AN ELECTION YEAR! Also point out if you are so useless, worthless, and ineffective as they make you out to be, why in HELL are they so afraid of you staying in office? So you can do nothing more to upset them? Totally illogical! They are so afraid that you and WE will get re-elected and finish the things that we set out to do in 2008 – and they are scared to death that will take away from their comfortable life they have created for themselves or will take away the corporate power they have amassed that keeps them in power and in control of everything. <u>They know they have nothing to sell to the WE THE PEOPLE MIDDLE CLASS</u>, and have even less interest in actually doing anything for the middle class! <u>That is what the 2008 election was all about and what this election should be all about as well!</u> <u>THE CLASS WARFARE THEY BLAME ON YOU, THEY ACTUALLY STARTED BEFORE REAGAN!</u>

Nail the oil prices on their support from big oil, Wall St, pharma and insurance companies! As Matlock always said about his trial wins, "Only a reasonable doubt is all you need"! <u>Put them in the REASONABLE DOUBT shadow of their own support system and let the American public nail them to the cross for being total hypocrites on being for WE THE PEOPLE in their goals and agenda</u>. The more they make huge noises about your speeches, <u>the more you know you have hit a nerve and exposed their true agenda to public scrutiny and forced them to defend and obfuscate to cover it up!</u> They need to be exposed to a lot more and <u>let Clinton do it</u>. You are self serving when you do it. Some one else has to do it for you! <u>When you hit a nerve start drilling in on it until they can no longer make up CRAP TO DEFEND IT! THEN MOVE ON</u>!

<u>The GOP vision of the American DREAM is based on houses! Six houses in the posh locals of this country, a car elevator for eight cars and our houses in FORECLUSURE</u>! Our houses in foreclosure good for the GOP? You bet! The less you have to support the opposition and the more you are in debt, the better they are <u>able to sell the "OLD SONG" that less taxes are good for you and that we must reduce the deficit or be in huge trouble like Greece</u>! Forget that it was a European equivalent to GOP that caused the Greek crisis as well as the conveniently generated crisis here in America! All part of the Greed Over People's (GOP) Perfect Trap see at perfectrap.com

Note to President Obama, 4/22/12

First of all, a repeat of a reminder that I have given you constantly over the past 4 years! Being an educator of adult students, <u>I cannot over estimate the power and effectiveness</u> of CHARTS of employment, GRAPHS, LISTS OF YOUR ACCOMPLISHMENTS AS WELL AS COMPARISONS TO YOUR OPPONENTS/GOP IN GENERAL OVER THE PAST 15-20 PLUS YEARS. THESE MAKE THE CASE AND MAKE THEM STICK FOR A LONG TIME! Make simple one page (FRONT AND BACK) handouts that they can take home and share with friends as well as those they know who are duped by the opposition! Use full color RED for GOP crap, Blue for your accomplishments. Give them visual clues that stick to the psyche! They have been duped a lot!

You might ask at your rallies questions like the following: (The best education and most readily remembered is when you ask them to participate, because that truly engages their minds and locks them into the argument) "Have we all become a Nation of masochists?" "Have we fundamentally become the habitual victims of situations similar to wife beating? "Why do we seemingly rush back into situations of horrendous and constant abuse?" "Do you really want your salaries systematically reduced <u>another</u> 5% to 25% - and many 100% when those of the elite GOP will simultaneously go up 400%?" "Do you really want to return to a regime where your home values will go down another 15% to 35% and in many, many cases 100% in foreclosures?" "Do you really want to have your now dwindled savings and retirements reduced another 25%-50% or in many cases 100%?" Do you think these things JUST HAPPENED BEFORE? You think these things were not planned decades ago? <u>No</u>, you voted for the ReCorpiCONS that caused these events – on purpose! These were no accidents or simple incidental misfortunate incidents. <u>These were planned and are still being planned by the elite of the GOP party with the Right Wing and Tea Partiers being duped co-contributors to the goal.</u> YOUR LOSES ARE THEIR GAIN! I repeat because it is so important. <u>YOUR LOSES ARE THEIR GAIN!</u> They are the ones who have the money to buy up your now distressed properties at 10 cents on the dollar! But more powerfully than this, <u>they have put you in a LOT OF HURT</u> where you no longer have any monetary political power because you are just struggling to get by on far too little! And even more powerfully than that, is that your HURT FEEDS RIGHT INTO THEIR BOGUS ARGUMENT THAT TAX CUTS (GENERIC) ARE GOOD FOR YOU AND THUS THE NATION! YOU NEED EVERY DOLLAR YOU CAN GET! THEY CAN THEREBY MAKE THE CASE TO STARVE THE GOVERNMENT TO DEATH ALONG WITH SS, MEDICARE, POLICE ETC. <u>ala Grover Norquist</u>! This is POWERFUL stuff!

Stop and think over the past 14 years about who actually helped you and in particular during the worst possible of times – created by the ReCorpiCONs! Try to list things that the GOP actually did for you or America or WE THE PEOPLE during that time! Lets see, <u>NO JOB GROWTH THROUGHOUT THE BUSH YEARS.</u> TWO UNPAID FOR WARS THAT MADE THE RICH RICHER <u>paid for on time on the backs of our children, grandchildren and great grandchildren</u>! 800,000 JOB LOSSES/MONTH FOR TWO YEARS BEFORE OBAMA TOOK OFFICE – A TOTAL LOSS OF OVER 8-12 MILLION JOBS! FINANCIAL CRISIS just SHORT of

54   the GREAT DEPRESSION of 1939 ALSO A ReCorpiCON creation! Squandering a $5 trillion Democrat created surplus and running it into a $10.7 trillion deficit!! A ReCorpiCON deregulation caused banking crisis of unprecedented magnitude and ominous portent that threatened to destroy the nation that <u>WE THE PEOPLE were asked to bail out with whatever few dollars we had left</u>!

Not bad enough that we had to suffer tremendously/ endlessly from those PRIOR huge indiscretions, that we would longingly, like lemmings running for the cliff, run for the very people who created that disaster - AGAIN on the "promise" that they KNOW HOW TO FIX IT AND <u>WILL FIX IT FOR YOU 'THIS TIME' INSTEAD OF WHAT THEY DID TO YOU 'LAST TIME'</u>? IS IT NOT CLEAR TO YOU BY NOW <u>THAT THEY NEVER HAD IT IN MIND</u> TO DO ANYTHING GOOD FOR THE MIDDLE CLASS OR WE THE PEOPLE? HAVE YOU NOT SEEN THE LEGISLATION THAT THEY HAVE TRIED TO ENACT IN THE HOUSE? More than 29+ LAWS TRYING TO CONTROL WOMEN'S RIGHTS AND NOT ONE JOBS BILL – THAT IS THEIR RECORD SINCE TAKING THE HOUSE. Look at their VOTER SUPPRESSION laws passed in many states by ReCorpiCON controlled houses and governorships. How many of their <u>FAVORITE THINGS</u> do we have to ENUMERATE FOR YOU TO UNDERSTAND that it really doesn't matter if its GINGRICH or ROMNEY! THEY ARE NOT FOR YOUR GOOD WILL OR WELL BEING! <u>ON YOUR SIDE</u>, YOU HAVE THE ADVANTAGES OF <u>ROMNEY'S</u> HEALTH CARE BILL THE CREDIT CARD RIGHTS BILL, THE FINANCIAL REFORM BILL TURNING JOBS AROUND TO 4.6 MILLION INCREASE IN PRIVATE SECTOR, STOCK MARKET BACK OVER PRE 2006 DAYS, ETC.! GREAT JOB!

Note to President Obama 4/29/12

First of all, YOU MUST USE THE "ASK THE AUDIENCE QUESTIONS" TECHNIQUE to GET THEM INVOLVED & to "OWN" THE PROCESS!! I SEE MITT ROMNEY IS USING IT VERY EFFECTIVELY AT EVERY SESSION. I HAVE ONLY BEEN TALKING ABOUT THIS VERY AFFECTIVE TECHNIQUE FOR OVER 5 YEARS NOW! NOW JUST <u>USE IT LIBERALLY</u>!!

Let me give you a couple of parables that you may use, or hopefully find better ones to use effectively in your campaigns to get the <u>message across so effectively and memorably that no one will ever forget them</u>! They must stick to not just the candidates, but the entire GREED OVER PEOPLE party! YOU SEE, YOU, AND WE, ARE NOT RUNNING AGAINST ROMNEY, BUT THE ENTIRE <u>ReCorpiCON party, State & National philosophy and agenda</u>! It is their defining agenda, goal & methodologies that are the very Ockham's razor, the true tipping point of our time and that of the future that clearly shows that they are only for themselves and the very privileged 1%! The difference between the GOP and a dictator who uses overwhelming force to keep a dissatisfied dissident population <u>"in line", to stay in power, is a very miniscule difference indeed</u>!

Parable 1: Remember the "protection" schemes of the SE and other parts of the country a few years ago? A group of people come to your business and "suggest" that you might be wise to buy some "protection" insurance in case your business might burn down, get robbed, or vandalized. You tell them, that you already have fire and theft insurance so you don't really need any of theirs. Oh you guessed it, "just by accident" your business is vandalized and you have significant losses – as well as losses due to down time getting it back in shape for business. Your "own" insurance doesn't really help in these areas. It seems that you have a stream of just such bad luck – that is until you finally buy their "protection" insurance. It just happens to turn out that those who "accidently" burned down your business – ARE JUST THE ONES YOU <u>NOW</u> NEED TO SUDDENLY GET YOUR BUSINESS BACK ON TRACK/ PROFITABLE. <u>Sound familiar, now</u>?

Parable 2: Some people come to your town & your home or farm are "accidently" burned to the ground, all the factories (owned by them) you worked for in town shuts down and sends all the jobs to Asia, and the bank, (owned by them) has a huge loss and your savings & retirements are lost or greatly diminished! A couple of years later, <u>after they stop every attempt by good meaning people to try to help you</u>, they come back and, seeing your plight say to you, "My, my, look how badly you are doing! Look how bad things seem to be going for you now. Seems like <u>your friends</u> aren't able to do much to help you! Perhaps you should try a different set of friends, who <u>KNOW</u> HOW TO HELP YOU A LOT! If this happened to you, human nature being what it is, <u>you would BUMS RUSH that crowd out of town "on a rail"</u>!

However, since they actually seem to be a different set of people, or you don't recognize them personally from before, or they have new names like (Bain of your Life), GRINGRINCH, SANITORIUM, etc. instead of HW OR GW SHRUB, YOU <u>MAY BE FOOLED INTO THINKING THAT THEY REALLY ARE DIFFERENT PEOPLE AND DO CARE</u>!!! Do YOU NOT REMEMBER THE FIRST HALF OF THIS PARABLE? <u>THEY</u>

ARE THE VERY SAME ONES WHO BURNED YOUR HOUSE DOWN, SENT YOUR JOBS TO ASIA & BANKRUPTED YOUR SAVINGS AND RETIREMENT ACCOUNTS – NOT MERELY BY "ACCIDENT" BUT VERY DEFINITELY "ON PURPOSE"!

Why would they do such a thing? By doing this, they implemented several TOTAL advantages over you! One, instead of you being very profitable and secure in your life and jobs, you are now very needy & destitute – desperately needing all the help you can get to get by. Two, you no longer have any MONETARY political clout to defend yourselves against any further onslaughts that they may want to bring on you! (See First Parable) Three, you have no MONETARY power to mount an effective campaign against their huge MONETARY RESOURCES that are able to win all elections and therefore being able to bring down further reigns of terror upon you –> far worse than before because they are empowered and enabled! And four: when they come riding in on the great white horse and decry that they are your savior, you are desperately in need & are tempted to believe that they really mean it and intend to help you! Remember the 1% and the 99%? ROMNEY IS THE 1% AND ALL THE REST OF US ARE THE 99%! DOES THAT NOT DEFINE THE EQUATION FOR ALL TIME, ALL SITUATIONS, NAMES AND FACES? Keep in mind their design and goals! Being a republican, I have seen their goals and designs for America and it is not a pretty one for WE THE PEOPLE!! Never forget Parable 2 & who did this to you!! Remember that they're the ones who brought this trauma on you in the first place. Are you so stupid to buy into THAT THEY ARE THE "ONES" WHO WILL BAIL YOU OUT?! OH, THAT IS TOTAL BULL SHIT & NONSENSE!

Note to President Obama, 5/7/12

<u>First a note for Joe</u> which he will fully understand! A <u>vote for Romney</u> is like the experience good friends of yours had when they were hired by DuPont! They interviewed in winter and sought and acquired a lovely home to live in. It was up Limestone Rd near Kennett Sq. – a lovely home. When the <u>Spring and summer came</u>, <u>buyer's remorse suddenly set in</u> (way too late) when they realized the awful choice they made moving in next to one or two mushroom farms. I think you will fully understand the significance of this true story and how <u>it relates to voting for the ambiguous, hail, hearty & well met – just talk a good line - Romney</u>!! <u>Buyers remorse can become the most devastating & destructive decimation of well being</u>!

Being at the forefront of "Just in Time", SAP and TQC manufacturing that built America in the 70's - 90's, I'm no novice to what built America's greatness and No novice to all the diverse and dispersive elements that have systematically destroyed American's manuf. greatness and prowess. Not the least of which is the reduction of the top tax rate over 90% in Americas heyday - the 50's – 60's to 72% under GOP's hero Reagan and now a mere 35% (if they pay it) and now they want to make it 25%! You know where that stops – ZERO. <u>IT HAS GOT TO BE STOPPED NOW! THIS is FUNDAMENTAL to OUR FUTURE</u>!

The only way to stop it is to get an all Democratically controlled House and Senates not only nationally, but in all state houses across the country – there has to be a total Democrat revolution and fervor like 2008 – no less and a hell of a lot more than in 2008! You, Joe and

Clinton are the vanguard to start that revolution & launch it successfully. You must or we all will be "DAMNED" TA HAUSROUND. You must be joined by as many others who are respected and influential (perhaps some of our best senators/reps that have been forced out of the national congress) can be brought to great advantage to bring the message that this is not just a pivotal moment in our history, but a precipitous moment for our future if we let even one GOP, Greed Over People, ReCorpiCON win one election anywhere. It must be made clear that it is not to TAKE TOTAL POWER for 1000yrs BUT RATHER TO SAVE THE ENTIRE FUTURE OF THIS GREAT NATION & RETURN IT AND SAVE IT FOR "WE THE PEOPLE"!

I have just read your latest "fund raising note" and I have just one question. How is it that you know what to say to me and the private base (many DC fliers say it like it is) yet, you pull back the punches too much when you talk to outside groups. YOU HAVE GOT TO TELL IT LIKE IT IS TO AMERICA – CONTANTLY! YOU HAVE GOT TO PROVE THAT YOUR ALBIGHT SLOW UPHILL PROGRESS BACK TO THE AMERICAN DREAM IS 100,000 TIMES BETTER THAN THE CRUSHING, DESTROYING, FALLING OFF THE GOP CLIFF THAT THEY HAVE PLANNED FOR AMERICA!!! YOU AND I KNOW THAT THE DEPRESSION WAS NO ACCIDENT NOR THE RESULT OF A FEW BAD APPLES. IT WAS A DESIGNED PLAN WITH THE PURPOSE TO BANKRUPT "WE THE PEOPLE", TO DESTROY THEIR POLITICAL CLOUT! IT WAS TO BANKRUPT AMERICA TO PROMOTE THEIR ENERGY GOALS & GIVE AN IMPETUS TO THEIR AGENDAS OF CUTTING TREASURED PROGRAMS THAT HAVE MADE AMERICA SO GREAT AND AT THE FOREFRONT VERY COMPETITIVE INTERNATIONALLY!

60   Let me look at some items you wrote in the "fund raising". You are being disingenuous when you say they are patriots and perhaps well meaning in what they say! <u>Tell it like it is</u> - they are pathological liars! <u>Tell it like it is!</u> Their mission is to get a few a hell of a lot richer off our public monies and funds and at the 99ers expense and for the rest to basically go to H___ or wherever one goes when they are broke, lose their homes and have no prospects for a real job! We have lost our retirements, savings at the GOP hands and if we still have a job it is at greatly reduced wages or if lucky at a minimum wage. <u>Ask the participants if they are better off with the GOP caused foreclosures, job loses, reduction in wages, loss of retirements, savings or future hope! Talk about that tax!</u>

The next line should be: "All boats rise when the tide rises and when all boats rise ALL have a much better living – including the Rich 1%". Keep in mind, <u>the rich's profits are a direct result of many workers having good jobs and making good money to live the good life and spend money on the goods the rich sell to make great profits for themselves</u>! The true root to the wealth at the top is tons of workers working everyday to make products to sell!

In line 12, you are fudging too much the real issue. It isn't <u>that they don't GET IT</u> but that <u>this is their agenda and true goal</u> or ideology that they have to sell <u>to make the take over of all power work</u>! It is not a learning curve for them, it is by design and part of their mantra and for them there is nothing to learn but to keep pushing on and pushing on. If they fail, they will just keep pushing the same old line, because that is the party line!! PERIOD end of STORY!

First line next page is great! Let me tell you about a True story, a friend went into emergency a year ago for a minor problem. In two days they almost killed her in the hospital. She ended in IMCU for 8 days where they were only then able to undue the damage that was caused! The bill was $117,000 or more. With the <u>GOP voucher</u>, the result would be ABSOLUTELY CERTAIN BANKRUPTCY and <u>TOTALLY WORTHLESS!</u> <u>With Medicare $1,750 – PRICELESS!</u> YOU MAY USE THIS EXAMPLE WITHOUT USE OF NAMES OR LOCATION. IT IS ABSOLUTELY TRUE AND REPRESENTATIVE OF THE ADVANTAGES OF KEEPING AMERICA OUT OF CERTAIN BANKRUPTCY WITH SOMETHING LIKE MEDICARE! ABSOLUTELY NECESSARY TO MAINTAIN AMERICA'S FUTURE!

For the rest of us about raising funds for your campaign, you have to realize that <u>most of us have been totally tapped out</u> - not by accident but by total design by the <u>Greed Over People</u> party!! They do not want us to be able to pay for your or any other Democrat's campaign while their "OTHER" class of citizens, ala Citizens United legislation from the Bench, has huge discretionary dollars to spend against you and the Democrats! This is not an accident but clearly by design! You've got to fight your <u>campaign against ALL of the GOP</u> not just some robotic, MAX HEADROOM that has absolutely no clue about who "WE THE PEOPLE" are or anything about THEIR STRUGGLES! This is the man who when asked if the "Middle Class" are those who make under $100,000 said "No the Middle Class are those who make $200,000 to $250,000 or less! That class is part of top 3% of earners in country AND CERTAINLY IS NOT PART OF MIDDLE CLASS! OUT OF TOUCH!

62 Note to President Obama -Father's Day June 16, 2012

You know in the past month+ I have had a myriad of arguments for you to present to defeat the <u>G</u>reed <u>O</u>ver <u>P</u>eople's hungry beast that is out to tear this great nation apart and down to a Greece, Spain, Italy or Ireland. Note that in France and probably in Greece, the reaction is to go toward a more growth based government. However, I have come to a malaise about everything and at the moment almost just don't care anymore. This is serious, because I have been an ardent supporter thru thick and thin having written & published 5 books. I'm working on the latest book supposed to be out next month called "Perfect Trap" <u>the GOP's two decade plan to execute the PERFECT TRAP to achieve total power for the next century</u>!

Everyday, I talk to workers and others about the demise from a ReCorpiCON led government. There are 2 out of 20 employees that are savvy but most do not even know that a crucial election happened on Black Tuesday 6/5/12 in WI. They are totally unaware of anything significant that can happen to them if this election goes the wrong GOP way! Most say that they are just tired of the constant harangue and spewing of "nothing" in the news. In fact they never watch or listen to the news!! America is so <u>under informed</u> except to the seemingly endless GOP propaganda and <u>out and out lies</u> that <u>tends to seep into the subconscious psyche</u>. It is as if America seemingly has nothing left to really live for except to have to work until they die for essentially no reason since the GOP raided their retirements and savings and <u>have taken their ability to actually enjoy life at all any more</u>!

Seemingly, this is the problem with our government of BY AND FOR "WE THE PEOPLE" at all levels – no one, no matter how "connected", has any influence over the outcome of our politics! Apparently politicians only listen to those who can provide <u>bucko bucks</u> or are on the "inside track" with the politicians themselves! We the public have zero influence on whatever happens, and, damnation upon damnation, if you lose, we will have even <u>less than zero influence on anything</u> because they only work for the 1% & have no interest in We The People!

Well, despite that long tirade, I will attempt to remember and point out some observations. I saw your entire speech in Ohio this week. You certainly said all the right things but you have got to get outraged about what they are doing <u>AND PLANNING</u>! You have got to raise your voice and spirit <u>and fire these people up!!!!!</u> YOU HAVE GOT TO <u>RUN AGAINST THE ENTIRE GOP PARTY</u> AND THEIR REAL GOALS AND AGENDAS FOR THE 1%ers and the hapless 99%ers – curiously known as <u>WE THE PEOPLE</u>!! This was Kerry's problem! He talked like he saw things purely intellectually! Even the Union leaders who spoke before his election night <u>put a hell of a lot more fire into their speeches and spoke with such passion</u>!!! I don't mean Tim Robbins, but you must get the point! When you listen to <u>(Bain or our lives) he is fired up</u>. He talks with passion about "how bad you have been for America" He makes a case to vote against you even <u>if they are essentially untrue or treading upon the discontent they generated in the past decade in order to make a case that you would be and thus you are a failure!!</u> <u>They created that FAILURE!</u>

64   YOU SEE, THESE BAD ECONOMIC CONDITIONS <u>WORK FOR THEM ON EVERY LEVEL AND EVERY ANGLE</u> – EVEN IF THEY HAD WON THE 2008 ELECTION!! HAD THEY WON, THEY WOULD HAVE USED THESE BAD TIMES AND ECONOMIC CONDITIONS PEOPLE FOUND THEMSELVES IN TO JUSTIFY A QUICK, DRASTIC, DRACONIAN REDUCTION TO THE ENTIRE GOVERNMENT AND THEREBY JUSTIFY A TAX CUT TO 25% LEADING TO A ZERO % TAX. HOWEVER, THEY CAN AND ARE USING THE VERY SAME ARGUMENT ON YOU SINCE YOU ARE IN POWER. <u>THIS IS CLEARLY A SITUATION THEY CREATED ON PURPOSE TO DRASTICALLY CHANGE THE ENTIRE WAY WE FEEL ABOUT OURSELVES AND HOW THIS NATION SHOULD GO FORWARD</u>!! See a familiar pattern in the Moneyed, conservative nation's solution for Greece? These bad economic times would have Greeced (pun intended) the wheels to their ultimate goal of taking away every progressive advantage America has fought for over the past century – SS, Medicare, Great Schools & education, Head start for kids, A better, more affordable health care system, Great Police, military etc. They seem to hate America and its successes – pure and simple! <u>They gathered immense wealth as a benefit</u> of the <u>common good paid for by We The People</u> and now figure they do not need any of that – infrastructure, great salaries for the MDDL class, manufacturing in US! NONE OF IT DO THEY NEED OR CARE ABOUT FOR AMERICA. <u>They only want to extract whatever last dimes we pay for and are available in public works, schools, police, jails, libs, utilities, etc.</u>! ALL OF THIS IS NOW QUITE CLEAR BY THEIR ACTIONS IN STATES LIKE WI, MI, OH, PA, FL, ETC. AND <u>THEY ARE SO BOLD AS TO MAKE NO BONES ABOUT IT!!</u> THEREFORE IT IS YOUR OBLIGATION TO MAKE THESE <u>GOP</u>

GOALS/AGENDAS quite CLEAR to the ENTIRE AMER. PUBLIC BY WHATEVER MEANS YOU HAVE AVAILABLE. THEY CANNOT REFUTE IT BECAUSE THEY, the GOP State Houses & THE HOUSE of REPS HAVE SPELLED IT OUT FOR everyone!

You must run against the entire GOP at all levels - local, state and federal government. Here is an example! If the so called "business creators" of the ReCorpiCONS have any concern for businesses in America then they must be concerned about productivity and therefore minimizing lost work hours and lost production that severely cuts into productivity! Yet, one of the biggest losses to business is sick time, sick days off and the consequences of fearing to take action early when symptoms arise - out of fear of finding you must face a long lost time from work and therefore, wages! When people are uninsured, they fear about getting sick to the extent that they have to lose days at work and thus earnings. As a result they come to work when they shouldn't and infect a number of other people so the loss is multiplied many times. Therefore, if they were truly concerned about American Business, a reasonable national health care system that reduces sick time off/losses should be one of their highest priorities – unless they want 35 million people to just die and go away! That reduces the tax base if that is true. They use "fear of future" to make a case that their glib talk about you are not creating enough jobs and they can just magically produce 12 million more jobs will be a piece of cake for them! People in trouble will and do believe in this pure garbage, because they are so desperate that they need a savior! They kept you from being that savior by blocking everything you tried to do to create jobs and

66   a better economy at the street level! They, in accord with their "__PERFECT TRAP__" are trying to capture the election at all levels based upon the tremendous damage they <u>deliberately caused</u> to this great nation! Frankly, we all feel that we no longer have any future and that our children and grandchildren have none either – all in accord with their <u>PERFECT TRAP</u>!! See what the Book's frontage page says about the lead-ins to the "PERFECT TRAP": <u>Two unpaid for wars; Unpaid for Medicare part D; Unpaid for $3 trillion tax cuts for the rich; Unregulated OTC Derivatives that Brooksley Born warned about in 2005-2006 before she was shut down by Greenspan; taking a $5 trillion surplus from Clinton and running up a $10.7 trillion DEFICIT before you took office; Unregulated energy companies that, at the least, caused multi-trillion dollar losses to the Gulf not to mention the permanent destruction of the Gulf; Other Mine disasters costing millions; more secret executive orders than ever in the history of the country; more pork barrel than anytime in our history; more filibusters in the Senate than filibusters for all time! The beat goes on and on and on!</u>

This was all put on our children's & grandchildren's credit cards and is now being blamed on you as being the real culprit that is keeping America back! WHAT A LAUGH!!

Fundamental facts that you MUST GET ACROSS! When a family is in trouble financially, what do they do or can do? Yes, they can cut back a little on food, consolidate shopping trips to use less gas, use less toothpaste, turn the heat down a little in winter and use fans instead of air conditioning in summer. Most people have already long since done all those things. What they all need and seek almost immediately is more revenue (perhaps in the form of a job for the wife, or moonlighting)!!! LET ME REPEAT THAT AGAIN – THEY SEEK OUT <u>MORE REVENUE</u> - IN THE CASE OF GOVERNMENT THAT IS <u>TAXES</u>, NOT ON THE MIDDLE CLASS OR POOR WHO HAVE ALREADY PAID THE GREATEST PRICE FROM THE RECESSION AND HOUSING DEBACLE BUT FROM <u>THOSE WHO BENEFITED MOST SO ROYALLY, SIGNIFICANTLY FROM THE COMMONS THAT WTPL PAID FOR ALL THESE YEARS FOR THEIR DIRECT BENEFIT! SINCE THEY HAVE DANCED THE DANCE SO ROYALLY, IT IS NOW TIME FOR THEM TO PAY THE PIPER!!!</u> Simply put, it is their time to pay down the debt they created and benefited from directly!! It is time for them to pay their fair share. It is time for them to <u>pay back to America a small percentage of the horrendous gains they made creating the greatest debt in our history</u>!! As they say in the media, <u>PAY UP DEADBEAT!</u> <u>(Bain of our lives)</u> is not the answer unless he has to pay up at 35% instead of 13%. He is clearly not the answer - a slug should win against him, but he is glib and makes you look bad! <u>All THIS IS PART OF THE PERFECT TRAP PLAN THEY CREATED YEARS AGO! A GOP vote ENSURES we all LOSE!!!</u>

Talk about the Supreme Court and what will happen if they get into office! <u>A vote for a GOP ensures we all LOSE!</u>

When people work, they not only pay taxes, the company also pays more taxes but most importantly of all, the owners make larger profits – so everyone wins! More taxes pays down the debt faster. Therefore, the GOP should be anxious for more people to get back to work as soon as possible, but their actions in the past three years and especially after 2010 clearly shows they

68   intend to put their political interests well before the American people who they are sworn to support! They have no intention of creating more jobs while Obama is in office! Working people also buy more goods and that is a rising spiral that clearly works for EVERYONE!! THEY HAVEN'T PASSED ONE JOBS BILL SINCE 2010 BUT THEY SEEM TO WANT TO REGULATE A WOMAN'S VAGINA WITH MORE THAN 29 BILLS IN THE HOUSE!! FOR A PARTY THAT CLAIMS THEY WANT LESS GOVERNMENT INTERFERING WITH PEOPLE'S LIVES AND LESS REGULATION, THEY SURE ARE HELL BENT ON REGULATING EVERY ASPECT OF OUR LIVES AND OUR ABILITY TO VOTE OR RUN OUR SCHOOLS - THUS OUR ENTIRE LIVES!!! THEY ARE TOTAL HYPOCHRITES!

When schools go private, "public schools" lose big time. Does anyone stop to realize that when your "used to be public" schools go private, there is no local control anymore, no PTA, no local control of curriculum, who writes the text books, what propaganda is included in the teaching, who really shapes what is taught and is not taught!! (Remember un-intelligent design, No such thing as Global warming and scads more.) Ever think about that? Well you had better! And the bottom line, when things don't go well for the schools, guess what, they then raise our taxes to pay for their mistakes and botched job of running the schools. We then have no recourse – we are at the receiving end of a true dictatorship telling us what to do, how to think, not only when to jump but how high and who to pay for "THIS PRIVILEDGE"! BULL SHIT, THE FRAMERS OF THE CONSTITUTION INSISTED ON UNIVERSAL, PUBLIC EDUCATION SO THAT ALL BOATS COULD BE RAISED EQUALLY, NOT JUST PRIVILEDGED BOATS & THE REST ALL

<u>SINK! I have never seen such a truly Anti-American agenda as the one that 's created this crisis on purpose!</u>

When they privatize jails, all sorts of fraud, police/ judges on the take to keep the jails filled to overcapacity to ensure the taking of as much public money as is possible will occur. You see a public jail privatized will always cost at least 30% more than the public one because of profit motive. If they make it cost even more, then guess what, the "public" has to pick up the tab for the private owners of the "public good"! Privatize libraries and no new books will ever be bought which destroys the profit!

What is this exactly? It is <u>their way of taking every last nickel and dime we have in the form of "government" paying</u> for privates taking all the money. <u>They already took our salaries, our jobs, our homes, our savings and our retirements, so what is left is SS, Medicare, schools, Jails, Libraries, Utilities, police, firemen & now entire tax bases called cities and towns!!! It they win there's simply nothing left for us, for WE THE PEOPLE, THE AMER. DREAM OR THOSE GOOD OLD HEY DAYS OF THE 50-60'S!! GONE, GONE, GONE FOREVER, IRREVERSIBLY, NO GOING BACK!!!</u>

I hear you saying this is a "unique point in time where we must pick a path for the future". <u>YOU HAVE GOT TO SAY THAT WITH SO MUCH PASSION & CONVICTION & SO MUCH FIRE IN YOUR BELLY, SO MUCH CHARISMA THAT EVEN THE MOST HARDENED GOP WILL YELL "HALLELUJIA"</u>! This is no play thing, <u>THIS IS FOR KEEPS</u>!! You may go off on your great retirement and lecture series, but we who have been <u>MORTALLY WOUNDED</u> out here have less than no

70 options. NEVER FORGET THAT! IF YOU LOSE WE ARE ALL SCREWED! I MAKE NO APOLOGIES FOR THE LANGUAGE!!!

Part of the PERFECT TRAP is that we as the opposition are so broke we have little to no discretionary money to fight back. YES, THIS IS A PRE-PLANNED PART OF THE PERFECT TRAP! KEEP IN MIND I HAVE BEEN A REPUBLICAN ALL MY LIFE AND I HAVE SEEN THEIR PLANS, AGENDA AND GOALS FOR THE FUTURE! THIS IS NOT JUST A CONSPIRACY THEORY, IT IS THE GOALS THAT THEY HAVE PLANNED FOR WELL OVER TWO DECADES!

BOTTOM LINE: THOSE WHO CLAIM/WANT A SIMPLER, SMALLER, LESS INVASIVE GOVERNMENT ARE THE MOST "PANTS ON FIRE" HYPOCRITES OF ALL TIME! YOU SEE FOR THEM THERE ARE TWO DISTINCTLY SEPARATE CLASSES OF "PEOPLE" IN THE UNITED STATES. THOSE REAL, LIVE, LIVING PEOPLE WHO ARE THE WE THE PEOPLE OF THESE UNITED STATES, TO THEM THEY ARE OF ABSOLUTELY NO VALUE ACCEPT AS A GOOD SOURCE OF FUNDS! BUT OTHERWISE WE ARE SOMETHING TO CONTROL AND REGULATE THE HELL OUT OF! THE FAUX PEOPLE, CORPS WHICH WERE NOT EVEN INVENTED AT THE TIME OF THE CONSTITUTION, THEY WANT TO DEREGULATE COMPLETELY & NOT CONTROL AT ALL!

WHAT IMMEDIATE CONCLUSION SHOULD 99% AMERICA THEN DRAW? THE GOP IS ONLY FOR THE CORPS AND THE 1% AND THEREFORE TOTALLY AGAINST AND ABSOLUTELY NOT FOR WE THE PEOPLE AND CANNOT BE EXPECTED TO DO ANYTHING FOR THEM DESPITE THEIR SPEECHES AND PROTESTATIONS TO THE CONTRARY!

Absolutely urgent note to President Obama 6/23/12

I heard an analysis this morning about which <u>vision</u> to follow to avoid a new fiscal crisis leading to going off the ultimate cliff. I kept hearing about a "hole" in one regard or another and the epiphany came to me. Any drastic <u>cut in government spending will take this country right into the proverbial "hole"</u> so that <u>if it does occur the "hole" will actually make it essentially impossible to recover</u>! The "hole", by definition, will be VERY CASH SHORT!!! That is the essence of the <u>ReCorpiCON vision</u> for our future. They have already, by causing budget and debt limit extension fiascos last summer, caused huge loses in public employment in at the very least the state and local economies if not on the Federal basis as well. That in itself has not contributed to the economy, but rather worsened it. I am reminded of the gas shortage of the 70's where everyone was supposed to cut back on gas and heating oil. For those who were extravagant before, that was OK, but for my parents who had already cut heat back to the bone years before, it was impossible to comply! The same thing applies to the Government. If it is fat and cash abundant, it can take up the slack. But when it is already cut to the bone, there's no more room to give! <u>That's the situation they put us in</u>!

Just a note, the Sunday morning news shows as well as most other news shows now are abundantly sponsored by Oil and Gas Fracking companies. Guess what the message is! We NOW need Abundant (clean, safe – use, not production) energy that will power America's future growth and creation of millions of jobs. Then they have the <u>balls to say</u> that the <u>millions produced "could" be</u>

used to fund schools, police, other services. Note the word "could". Since they pay almost no taxes on huge profits, it is the misleading way to dupe the American public into thinking de-regulation of these would be good for Jobs in America! Only if there were jobs left in America that needed energy to grow, which at this time, we are not energy short! Another note, their commercials are now three minutes to one minute of news. It is clear that mass media is now doing what the government absolutely needs to do – RAISE REVENUES TO PAY FOR IT'S OPERATION – THAT MEANS RAISE TAXES TO SAVE US ALL!

WE THE PEOPLE have already paid for this very deep depression with loss of salaries, homes, wages, jobs, and added burdens on our schools and local government services. Many senior citizens have had to pay double additionally after the fact for things local and state legislatures have ginned up to recover their budgets! It's now time for those who benefited most from our losses/government bankruptcy to pay for all the damage they caused to the smooth running of our govern out of all their bonuses, salary increases & great perks we paid for!

What is it that institutions, small business, larger businesses, huge TV networks, do to survive hard times – WORK HARDER TO INCREASE REVENUES, SPEND MORE MONEY ON STIMULATING THE GROWTH OF THE BUSINESS and WORK TO FIND NEW SOURCES OF REVENUES! THEY PUT A LOT MORE MONEY INTO ADVERTISING AND SALES TO INCREASE REVENUES! THERE ARE MORE THAN TWO THINGS A GOVERNMENT CAN DO FOR THIS: PAY FOR A STIMULUS & RAISE TAXES ON THOSE WHO BENEFITED MOST SO THEY CAN PAY for it! IT TAKES MONEY TO MAKE MORE MONEY!

Look at the contributors to the (Bain of our lives) campaign & ask yourself, which one of these people or orgs. are ones who would help us (the WE THE PEOPLE)? NOT ONE OF THEM!! Are any of them people who would even want to know any of us? ABSOLUTELY NOT, THEY LOCK US OUT OF THEIR GATED COMMUNITIES SO THEY NEVER HAVE TO DEAL WITH US!! THEY LOOK AT US WITH HORRENDOUS DISDAIN & CONTEMPT!! Not one of them has any interest in the 99% of these United States, except as a group to further exploit and control and RAPE OUR EARNINGS, TAXES, JOBS AND SAVINGS! ALL OF THEIR "PROMISES" ONLY SERVE TO WIN THIS ELECTION SO THEY CAN DO EXACTLY WHAT THEY HAVE ALWAYS WANTED TO DO – DECREASE THE TRULY USEFUL PART & INCREASE THE CONTROLLING PART OF GOVN AND PAY EVEN LESS FOR THAT WHICH THEY HAVE DIRECTLY BENEFITED & HAVE US PAY FOR CONTROLLING THE HELL OUT OF US! Who do they all know and work with? EACH OTHER LIKE AN EXCLUSIVE CLUB! What has the ReCorpiCON party always supported --The rich and corporations! They have all made huge fortunes off the backs of 99% of the country who worked for peanuts to make their huge fortunes! Do you think that it will be these people and organizations that will now suddenly turn and save MAIN ST? GUESS AGAIN, (I HAVE A BRIDGE FOR YOU IN ALASKA), GUESS AGAIN! NO!!!!!! They have ZERO interest in our plight, struggles, SAD CASES and futures! Eric Hovde, Rep from WI, had the balls to complain that the news media was spending way too much time on People's plights, struggles, and economic sad stories and not enough on "the real issue" of national debt and lack of jobs! HOW MANY JOBS BILLS HAVE THEY PASSED SINCE 2010? ZERO!!!! HOW MANY VAGINA

74 **REGULATION BILLS** HAVE THEY PASSED IN THE SAME TIME? **WELL OVER 29**!!

Ask the crowd, "<u>Name one thing</u> the GOP did for you (WE THE PEOPLE) in the past 12 or last 3 years"! Yes, name just one and I bet even the hard core bottom/middle level GOPS cannot name <u>EVEN ONE</u>!! Then, when they cannot, start naming a list like, Two wars put on ours and children's credit cards, Medicare part D put on ours and children's credit cards, $3 trillion tax cut for the rich put on our and children's credit cards, "No child left behind", which in itself is an abomination designed to dummy down America, but more importantly was never paid for either!! The list goes on and on and on! All of the crap they caused to bankrupt all of us was "said to be paid for out of the incredible jobs that they would create"! There is <u>NOT ONE JOB!</u> You on the other hand provided affordable health care for almost all of America that essentially paid for itself from savings and better policing. We killed Osama Bin Laden, a Shrub ally, he apparently never intended to kill. We passed the financial regulation bill to help prevent a re-occurrence of what happened in 2007-2008. <u>Name just one thing the (Greed Over People) party did for America</u>? Hey, <u>I'm listening here & nothing!!!</u>

So what are the only things the <u>ReCorpiCON party has always been totally supportive of</u>? It is the rich, huge corporations and now multinational corps. <u>When have any of them been supportive of the 99% WE THE PEOPLE</u>? So why would any of these organizations who have historically exploited us for their own huge gains, salaries and profits, <u>suddenly have a keen interest in helping us all get jobs and again have an American Dream</u>? Within

2000 – 2008 years, <u>they have built the perfect THIRD world country</u>! Why in HELL would they want to change that? This is perfect for them so do you think that they or (Bain or your lives) has any real interest in changing that direction? HELL NO!! It works so well for them and <u>their Corporate Handlers so why would they want to stop it</u>?!!

We should not grind salt into the already abundant wounds of 99% of We The People who were neither instigators nor willing partners in this horrendous insult to the economy of the entire United States government and most of the We The People! What happened was not incidental, accidental, "just happened", a mere mishap or just an oversight but a deliberate, planned act to make fortunes for the top 1% at the total and complete expense of the bottom 99%. <u>WE ALREADY PAID our fair share, THE PRICE IN SPADES FOR THE DELIBERATE GREED OF A FEW</u>!! WE HAVE ALREADY SACRIFICED FAR MORE THAN ANYONE RICH OR POOR SHOULD HAVE TO, TO TRY TO ELEVIATE THE MESS THEY CREATED! <u>AND YET, WE HAVE ALREADY PAID ADDITIONAL AMOUNTS AND LOSSES IN ESSENTIAL SERVICES AS A DIRECT RESULT OF THE HORRENDOUS DISASTER THAT A SMALL FEW HAVE CREATED FOR PROFIT, GREED AND TOTAL POLITICAL POWER OVER US</u>. I HAD TO PAY OVER $20,000 FOR A CHANGE IN COVENENT WITH THE STATE THAT THESE ReCorpiCONS DIRECTLY CAUSED! <u>I AND THE REST OF THE 99% DO NOT HAVE THAT KIND OF DISCRETIANRY MONEY TO SPEND ON ANYTHING</u>!! WE DON'T EVEN HAVE ENOUGH MONEY TO JUST GET BY FROM MONTH TO MONTH, LET ALONE HAVE A SMALL ENJOYMENT – AND THEY WANT TO TAKE MORE AND MORE & MORE <u>without PAYING even a SMALL TOKEN from</u>

76   the VAST RICHES they gained IN THIS DELIBERATELY CREATED DISASTER! Such Hubris! If you didn't see "America Now"- "Lost in the Suburbs" on NBC "dateline" on Sunday, 6/24/12 you should have one of your people watch it and report on it! It was about three families that were well educated and well jobbed that all lost their jobs and were soon on welfare, food stamps, food banks and humiliation, separation, loss of homes and living on the street. This isn't just about the poor, who have been lost long ago in this process - it is about the Middle Class that is totally at risk! GOP's time to pay their FAIR SHARE!

You lose your job for as little as 6-9 months and you are no longer viable in your field and a hiring risk! I know, I have been there. You are forced to take a job at Ace or McDonalds with no chance of getting out of that level after that. You're then eternally doomed to a whole level or two below where you are trained and had bucko experience - for the rest of your lives! Therefore, a small part (the part the media mentions occasionally) of this "Deliberately Created" disaster is the economic disaster to the Nation and 99% of the population. Business, stock market and corp. profits recovered long ago. The huge part is the permanent loss of a generation or more of brilliant minds, scientists, innovators, manufacturing experts, managers, creators, true job creators and company founders. This happened in China when Mao sent all the scientists and intellectuals out to commune farms all over China for a few years. In that short time, the disastrous effect was a loss of two or three generations of scientists and intellectuals because the institutions die, the supporting infrastructure goes away, ROLE MODELS

THAT INSPIRE the NEXT GENERATIONS are GONE! It's a FAST SPIRAL DOWN THAT TAKES GENERATIONS TO REBUILD. ONE DOES NOT BUILD GREAT INSTITUTIONS IN JUST A COUPLE OF YEARS! IT STARTS IN GRADE SCHOOL AND ALL THE WAY UP THROUGH POST GRADUATE STUDIES – OVER AND OVER & OVER AGAIN – requiring ROLE MODELS AND ORGANIZATIONS IN PLACE many years in the MAKING - WELL ESTABLISHED AND WITH GREAT REPUTATIONS!!!!!!

I just heard a (Bain of your lives) campaign talk in Virginia. He is using the questions and huge roaring response format very effectively against you. He is effectively defining the hell out of you. He is using your own promises and statements against you so effectively there is no doubt in those peoples mind that you caused everything bad and did not do anything to fix it. (I told you years ago before you were elected to use that format) Two problems: he is not giving any answers, except to replace you with himself. He is not revealing anything about himself or what he would do. Great for debates!

He looks like an alien in a strange land when he appears. He is so uncomfortable with the people he meets because they are totally foreign to him. He is just a caricature like a robot (looks exactly like Max Headroom), or a spokes person coached on how to relate to the buyer and what to say. He has no visible character, morals, standards, principles, vision – and will say anything and everything that satisfies the mood at the time and place. All I can say is I hope you are saving up all these isolated statements that he has made as a matter of convenience and will put them side by side in

78   multiple ads where they totally contradict each other & show what a total principle-less phony he is. Again, go after the entire GOP goals and agenda to tie him to the total destruction that most people realize happened in that 8 year total disaster under the SHRUB! You created all this damage in just three short years? Good luck on that! Get that fire in your belly and total indignant in your voice & rake the hell out of the entire Greed Over People goals and agenda! You have to define the HELL out of the GOP party and agenda! (Bain of Your Life) has taken so many sides on all the issues it would take 13 dimensional "String Theory" to even try to sort out the implications!

We've got to save America from a small, powerful, rich, elite force in America that would – as a result of a zealot following of an "ideal"- take us back to the dark ages, dismal past and inadvertent destruction of America - its real ideals, goals, glory, power, prowess and permanent place in the world! The only solution now is a return to a strong central government BY AND FOR WE THE PEOPLE to protect us from forces hell bent on taking total control (house, senate, president and Supreme Court) of not just our government but as a desired result ALL OF OUR LIVES AND WAY OF THINKING AND LIVING! Party of Freedom? HELL NO!! I don't mean a dictatorship – which is where they seem to be heading - but a government of WE THE PEOPLE that is supportive, encouraging, helpful in bad times, advancing ways that everyone can have a good life and a part of the American dream once again! That is the defining question you must put to the American public over and over again! WANT TO GO BACKWARD to Destruction or RUN FORWARD to a great FUTURE!!

Note to President Obama 7/21/12

Boy, I nearly fell off my chair when I heard you talk about things I thought about a couple of weeks before about how businesses don't just make all that money on their own merits but that they are the very fortunate beneficiaries of the <u>institutions and infrastructures that were supplied to them by govern't and others to great advantage to make them extremely successful and have the advantage when they compete globally</u>. Sorry you got beat up over it by the GOP, but you were dead on and America knows you were dead on in saying it! You might have punched it up more on the following facts. <u>All successful business at the very least did not train the talent that they hire that materially added to their success and profits.</u> <u>Most were trained at public expense in public funded universities, though even those trained at private institutions were largely supported by public funds & government contracts/research like at Stanford & MIT</u>. Keep in mind, <u>State Universities</u> like at Davis, CA <u>did fundamental research</u> on Wine chemistry and effective processes so that the <u>fledgling CA wine industry could begin to effectively compete & surpass long standing European wine countries!</u> There is no way a single winery could have been successful at doing that by themselves! OSU developed science of grass seeds to help Oregon farmers compete very well. Other states did similar things as well. Almost all manufacturing uses the Interstates, bridges, railroads, internet to move raw materials and product to customers and advertise and get orders. These were not free, the government had to pay for them, develop them or build them for their "free" use.

80   One would like to impound all of GE's trucks that use the highways because they pay zero taxes – therefore they do not pay for maintenance and upkeep of the highways they use to great advantage! Boy, do you think you would hear a stink from them if you did that? WOW! <u>Perhaps they would get the message that taxes and the common good are excellent for business!</u> America's heyday was in the 50-60's <u>when the tax rate was over 90%!!!!!</u> Business was <u>booming then and everyone was sought out and employed in high tech companies and had many many opportunities and a good life! Compare that to now!</u> <u>Low tax rate has built huge money disparity!</u>

The only companies that may barely qualify for doing it on their own, are the financial rip-off companies that don't use roads or bridges. They use someone else's money to extract money from all the rest of us! However, they do use the internet, air travel (regulated and protected by government) and people trained in public or private collages or universities. Since they produce nothing of value, they just don't count and should be made illegal or eliminated in some other way as wasters, spoilers, detractors of Democracy or spoilers of Society itself! They are truly bottom feeders & scum of earth! Getting back to (Bain of your Life), I think America is finally getting the view of his company as a true spoiler – not a job builder or creator! He wants to do it to America!

America is getting DAMNED Tired of the (Bain of your live's) kind of Silly <u>Business that has taken America artfully down the tube</u>. <u>It was that kind of "successful" businessman that tanked the middle class and the economy</u>! I don't care if (Bain of Your Life) is a so called "successful businessman" that in itself doesn't qualify him in any way or form to be President of the United States! That is pure bullshit. When you run a business, whether a rip off or legitimate job builder, when you say jump, everyone jumps at the same time and asks "how high?" As you know, when you are President of the USA, you are <u>quite often the tail of a huge dog that may wave you any which way at any time or for any purpose</u>. Yes, you lead, yes, you cajole, yes, you guide, yes, you negotiate, yes, you set a plan, yes, you set a direction, yes, you build alliances, yes, you seek compromise and common ground, yes, you set a vision, but in these times, the politics and the congress does the work (OR NOT). And if you are (Bain of your life) right now, whatever whim is blowing at the time, sets the current message or vision for perhaps all of 15 minutes before he changes it for some other whim. God help him trying to make this or any congress do anything that he says so confidently that he will do on the first day on the job - let alone anytime in the future. It's a wishy-washy, chameleon, pandering, jelly flip-flopper that swamps by orders of magnitude the flip-flopper they tried to pin on John Kerry. Look at the various videos of him only a few years ago – <u>that paint him in totally opposite directions to today</u>!

John Sununu made a huge case that America was built from the bottom up by entrepreneurs and small business owners - NOT TOP DOWN AS THE GOP INSISTS HAPPENS FOR THEM TO MAKE THE ARGUMENT THAT TAX CUTS FOR THE RICH AND POWERFUL CREATE JOBS! BULL SHIT! Their own spokesman refutes their TAX CUT PREMISE AS BEING FALSE! <u>Where do they get off claiming tax cuts for top</u>

82   <u>1-2% creates jobs when they apparently know that argument is false</u>? Totally ridiculous! Didn't work under Bush and not since extended after 2009. Besides, it is a <u>ZERO SUM GAME when the rich pay less, the Middle Class have to pay a lot more, run up a huge deficit or lose extremely essential services that makes America great!!</u>

If you are the ones who created this huge deficit and benefited from it royally, then you, GOP, need to pay for the damage you caused and created. PAY UP DEAD BEAT! TRUST ME, WE'LL TAKE CARE OF THAT LATER SAID THE WOLF IN SHEEPS CLOTHING, OR (BAIN OF YOUR LIVES) - THE SPIDER TO THE FLY. You are beginning to define (Bain of your life) very well. Keep pressure on the Tax forms for 99 – 2002 to get to the issue of was he at Bain or not during that time! The more he resists, the more America can speculate as to how bad it is. He is a terribly flawed individual and all of it is beginning to come out! See videos of how he bragged about getting all the govn money he could for Mass. See videos of how he bragged about getting over 410 million from Govn to fix Olympics in Utah & to pay off Utah business buddies that were on the hook! He even bragged about getting 1 million from Dept of Education to pay for tickets for school children to attend Olympics. Get all that stuff and put it in ads and that will sink his ship like a rock! What a total fraud he is! One wonders why the establishment of the GOP would even touch him as a viable candidate. It's now a toss up between Sarah and (Bain of your Life) as to who is the sleaziest and most risky candidate to present. No, I take it back, he's in the big leagues, Sarah is small potatoes compared to him. They must think unlimited Citizens

United money and states rigging elections will take care of the rest to defeat you. <u>You have got to get all of your people fired up as well as the independents and registered and out to vote</u> if you are going to win – there is no option, WE CANNOT LOSE OR LIFE ENDS! YOU HAVE GOT TO GET FIRE IN YOUR BELLY, <u>YOU HAVE GOT TO ASK PEOPLE TO GET INDIGNANT, TO GET ANGRY, TO GET REALLY MAD ABOUT ALL OF THE DAMAGE THE GOP AND THEIR CRONIES HAVE DONE TO ALL OF US, THE MIDDLE CLASS, THE POOR, THE MINORITIES, THE HISPANICS AND BLACKS.</u>

THIS FIGHT IS THE MOST MONUMENTAL FIGHT FOR SURVIVAL OF THIS NATION, DEMOCRACY AND WE THE PEOPLE OF THE CENTURY IF NOT OF THE MILENIUM! PERHAPS YOU DO NOT REMEMBER HOW DESPARATE A FIGHT IT WAS TO DEFEAT BOTH HITLER AND HIROHITO IN JAPAN. IT WAS A FIGHT TO THE DEATH OF A HELL OF A LOT OF AMERICANS AND WAS TOUCH AND GO FOR A VERY LONG TIME. AFTER PEARL HARBOR, THERE WAS <u>NO HALF WAY</u> ABOUT IT! IT WAS AN ALL OUT EFFORT TO THE END. THIS SURELY IS NOT HITLER, NOR HIROHITO, BUT THE CONSEQUENCES FOR AMERICA are ESSENTIALLY THE SAME and THE EFFORT TO KEEP THAT KIND OF TOTAL TAKE OVER OF OUR GOVERNMENT FOR AT LEAST 4 GENERATIONS IS NO LAUGHING MATTER!! THIS IS SERIOUS!!! <u>THE VERY EXISTENCE OF THE FOUNDING DEMOCRACY IS TOTALLY, IRREVERSIBLY AT STAKE HERE!</u>

Any time a group, a party, an ideology <u>IS</u> more interested in using whatever means and gaming of the system for taking total irreversible control of our "representative" government for an extended period of time exceeding 2 or 4 years RATHER THAN working for the good and well being of the majority of the citizens of this great nation & further putting at great risk the very foundation and credit worthiness of this nation, you have the very basis of domestic terrorism which clearly has none of the public interests at heart!! Vote No to the GOP!

By the way, I just saw your speech in Portland - Very rousing and to the point. You are beginning to give it some punch and are inspiring the crowd. You are stressing what you (and we) are about for the future and gave but a minimal definition of what THEY are about. Need to make their agenda a lot more clear – to stress how devastatingly destructive it has been & will be!!

Now for some ideas on things that may help to get the base & independents fired up! If you set up a series of sub sites on your main campaign site, or independent from it, that people can interact with & give you some effective feed back. One could be an open forum on having people try to give you ONE THING THE REPUBLICONS HAVE ACTUALLY DONE FOR THE MIDDLE CLASS AND AMERICA IN THE PAST 15 YEARS. ONE, YOU WILL EITHER HAVE NOTHING LISTED AND TWO YOU WILL HAVE THE DIE HARD GOP FEEBLY TRYING TO ADD SOMETHING THEY FEEL WAS A GOOD THING. IF THE SITE GETS ENOUGH PUBLICITY, IT WILL BECOME AN INTERESTING COMMENTARY ON THE DIFFERENCES IN THE TWO VISIONS OF THE FUTURE!

HAVE A SISTER SITE THAT LISTS ALL THE THINGS THE DEMS HAVE EITHER PROVIDED OR TRIED TO PROVIDE FOR THE SUCCESS OF THE MIDDLE CLASS AND AMERICA. YOU MAY

GET SOME GOP CREATED NEGATIVES HERE. THAT WILL BE SURELY RIDICULED BY YOUR SUPPORTERS.

THE BIG SITE WILL BE TO LIST ALL THE DAMAGE THE GOP HAS DONE TO THE MIDDLE CLASS AND AMERICA. Voter suppression, two unpaid for wars, Medicare part D unpaid for, Every Child left behind, attempts to destroy SS and Medicare. Unregulated Wall St. – financial collapse of America/world, Unregulated Energy companies, BP Gulf DISASTER, mine DISASTERS, fracking - causing water pollution and earthquakes, deadly oil refinery explosions, raping of the fine Appellations and river pollution, the Unfunding of Planned parenthood, etc. etc. etc. All of this needs to come out! There are so many disasters caused by the ReCorpiCON party that it is hard to conceive that any of them would consider showing their faces in public much less, bragging about "HOW THEY BURNED the FARM DOWN and NOW they know HOW IT WAS BUILT"! Does that, NOW, make them the experts to trust to REBUILD THE FARM THEY BURNED TO THE GROUND in the first place? WE THE PEOPLE, America, All have very serious doubts they are even a dubious choice to be considered to do that!

86   Note to President Obama   8/12/12

You all must have had the <u>Wet Dreams of your lives</u> when (Bain of your life) selected Paul Ryan for VP!

When I heard the news Saturday morning, I could not believe my ears! I <u>thought they learned their lesson with Sarah Palin</u>! Instead of picking a safe candidate like Portman, they pick the only Lightning Rod (next to Jindal) that could bring down the wrath of almost the entire country and lose their last safe haven, the independents. With this one move, they have essentially lost everyone they needed to win the election. What is more, if done right, this will also set the Ockham's razor between the ReCorpiCon House and Senate candidates versus the Democrats running against them! You see, <u>most of those TeaBaggers voted for the Ryan Budget in the House</u>. By the way, is it suddenly a tenant of the Mormon Church to lie about everything if it serves the end result? I would not think so! I'd think the Mormon Church would be upset by their fair-haired boy treading the boards – giving them a bad name!

Remember how often I talked about the ZERO SUM GAME of finance? If the rich pay less, either the middle class, poor, seniors, Hispanics must pay more to sustain the status quo, or lose out on the ESSENTIAL services that they desperately need to get by in these and forthcoming bad times. <u>A govrn doesn't run on charity, good hopes, well meaning wishes</u>! It runs on money that it must raise the only way it can, <u>through taxes</u>! If it doesn't raise taxes, <u>the money IN will always be less than the money OUT</u> – a fact the GOP are counting on as a way to take down the Federal Government! By preying on the too easy mantra of NO MORE TAXES, NO NEW TAXES, OR TAX THE RICH LESS AND THAT WILL CREATE JOBS AND PROSPERITY you have a formula that ensures the total destruction of these United States! Just show a chart of how they have successfully brought their tax rate down from over 90% in the 50's-60's, THE VERY HEY DAY OF AMERICA, to 35% (actually 15% for most rich 1%ers) and SHOW the results for America! Show comparative pictures of the great times versus the present disaster that we all face now and bring the point home with passion! This is not an election about a "smiley robot" and a "lightning rod" side kick promising each and everything to their "newly discovered" middle class "buddies" and how they will finally fix everything (they destroyed in the past decade) if WE will only vote for them!! It is about a philosophy to continue to tear down America, rape the middle class and poor, extract every last and future dime from them and walk away with the power to do this essentially forever! You have got to make this image of the ReCorpiCON party's agenda STINK to high heaven! It has to smell every time those candidates get up to speak, it has to STINK every time they put out an ad or a slogan, it has to stink every time they are seen or heard. Why? Because it does STINK to high heaven! Destroy it in great detail, take it apart and expose the hypocrisy at all levels! At least with "Robin" at his side, you have something concrete to shoot at! With (Bain of your Life) you had nothing to shoot at because he was all over the place and would never reveal a plan other than to complain about how badly you have been doing with your promises! Well ask him, with his new found interests in suddenly creating millions of jobs, fixing the plight of those in trouble from the ReCorpiCON created crash, WHERE IN HELL WERE THE ReCorpiCONs during the nearly past 4 years when the Democrats were begging them to help do something about the situation? PARTY OF NO, that's where they were! Party of Obstructionism. Party of passing 30 bills to regulate the vagina and not one bill to help create jobs! Just because there is a "smiley robot" face out there now trying to be concerned about the "new" friends of the MIDDLE CLASS, does not mean they have any intention of helping the middle class to anything more than further ripping off their moneys, loss of more jobs and perpetual poverty? It is just not in the ReCorpiCON best interests to have a strong middle class or a moneyed middle class!! They had that under Clinton and it nearly killed the GOP party! Not again for the GOP!

Talk about a welfare system without a work requirement! $3 trillion for the rich without paying for it other than at the direct expense of the middle class is a welfare system without a work requirement and a very expensive one at that! How do they get off paying themselves huge tax cuts at our expense? How does that reduce their trumped up huge deficit? How does that save this nation? It's all smoke and mirrors, but we've seen that "illusion" many times before starting with Reagan, Bush senior & now this bunch! IT JUST DOES NOT WORK! It never has and never will. When will the American public get over this propaganda notion that sending money to the rich that takes it off shore, will somehow magically produce jobs here in America? IT JUST AIN'T GOING TO HAPPEN, PERIOD! Now don't get me wrong, I'm not against people having a lot of money, big houses and big cars, etc. if they are doctors or small business owners who have worked hard and long hours to build that wealth. They earned it and hopefully they can enjoy it. No, what has got to be brought to light are the Greedy Bastards who <u>use our money to build huge amounts of wealth without taking any risk</u>! If it fails, we bail them out, if it makes tons of money, guess what, THEY TAKE the PRIZE AND WE ARE SHIT OUT OF LUCK !! NO MORE GOPS!

Note to President Obama   8/21/12

HOW MANY TIMES HAVE I TOLD YOU, <u>YOU ARE RUNNING AGAINST THE ENTIRE REPUBLICAN PARTY AND THEIR RTWNJ IDIOTIC, FREAKISH CONTROL FREAK IDEOLOGIES FOR THE TOTAL SUPPRESSION OF ALL OF AMERICA</u> – EXCEPT THEIR NEW FRIENDS NOW KNOWN AS 'PEOPLE' – CORPORATIONS - <u>THAT GET A FREE PASS!</u>

You are not just running against one awkward "ROBOT" with fake smile or a batman sidekick, who is so freakishly on the side of disaster for all, that he is just plain scary! At least Batman & Robin were for the common good! Even if you were to win against Batman and Robin, <u>if you do not kill the GOP SNAKE in the house and Senate, you will have 4 more years of tough times for America</u>. America cannot afford to go back to the 19th century – not after the past decade, <u>there is nothing left to go back to if that crowd gets into power!</u> They lie in every talk and every speech and the "liberal media" lets them get by with it! You cannot have a habitual liar as President of US – he already has no credibility in the world arena. If he wins and goes on doing what the GOP did in past decade, the American public will tear them up and spit them out – <u>but sadly too late. We cannot afford another Alito or Roberts on the court!</u> America has to be warned every time you campaign. <u>You must vilify the entire GOP party.</u> <u>Todd Akin is just the tip of the nut job iceberg when it comes to the GOP's dangerous ideologies and model for America.</u> There is no room for compromise with the ReCorpiCON party! <u>America can't survive even another 4 years of that total STUPIDITY, IDIOCY, FREAKISH out of touch cult-like beliefs about the state of the human condition!</u>

YOU HAVE GOT TO EXPOSE THE GOP NUT JOBS!

It is fortunate that TODD AKIN said what he said NOW as it <u>exposes the very underbelly of the entire ReCorpiCON party and their truly bizarre VIEWS OF AMERICA</u>. They lie to try to blend in with 99% of the PPL that they totally despise, hate, cannot tolerate, do not believe in or would want to associate with at any time! They are aloof and know so much better than WTPPL that they will lie to be elected in order to SAVE AMERICA FROM ITSELF! By the way, a Mormon friend of mine back when the Challenger blew up, told me that the <u>Mormon agenda is that they are the chosen ones to take over America and to save it from itself</u>. That was 20 years ago, and now they have found the "Savior" that they believe will do that job for them! Good luck on that! JUST "<u>DAMNED</u>"GOOD LUCK!

Note to President Obama   8/27/12

This is important for the Convention and perhaps before it starts! When there has been two consecutive RNC conventions diminished, overshadowed, marred or delayed by Hurricanes and the Katrina factor, the <u>GOP should by now understand the importance</u> of a strong, <u>supported and fully funded</u> Federal government that is the only entity large enough that spans more than one state that can deal with disasters of this magnitude! Note that Louisiana and Mississippi have already declared their states a national disaster area even before Isaac hits the region! Boy, those anti Federal Government focused southern governors are sure quick to grab federal help when they are the victims! Keep in mind it is NOAH, a federal agency, that predicts these storms and their most likely tracks days to weeks before they hit so that residents and local governments can be prepared long before disaster hits. Without that, they would be almost entirely at the mercy of the storm at the last minute to deal with a disaster. In the case of Katrina, they were warned 4 days before & basically ignored it almost completely. Oh yes, they do realize the benefits for them, <u>they just don't want to be the ones that pay for it</u>. After all, it's those common folks that are at risk so they should be required to pay for it! Just a bit disingenuous! Have they never heard of one of the oldest companies/corps, - the insurance co's? That is what insurance companies do – SHARE RISK among everyone NOT JUST THE POOR!

Now for the next subject, Medicare. <u>I'll repeat this true story</u> just one more time. A one day visit to the hospital turned into <u>a 10 day stay in ICU</u>. The <u>bill was $117,000</u>

which for anyone, even you the president, would be totally non manageable! With a Ryan voucher – it would mean certain bankruptcy & family disaster - WORTHLESS! With present Medicare, $1750 - manageable with time payments – PRICELESS!

The message to those over 60 is this! <u>There is no reason to change Medicare and its benefits</u>! If there is a funding problem the answer is in raising the rates at which it is extracted from paychecks to pay the premium. How many times do insurance companies do this with their policies? This happens actually quite often when the actuarial data shows that it is necessary. Other methods might include means testing for those whose net worth is over $1 million, for example where only catastrophic coverage (major medical) is covered for those whose net worth is over a certain amount. The $716 billion that the GOP crows about you taking out of Medicare, (when did any present GOP ever complain about saving or reducing costs by $716 billion?) but yet here it is and they are not only the ones who would have done the same thing but would have increased costs on the elderly in the process! What total Hubris and complete Hypocrites!

I'd like to know where the <u>RePubliCONs</u> were for the past 4 years when the economy was so bad and there was an even greater need for job creation? <u>They were the party of NO, the party of obfuscation and the party of obstruction</u>! Are they the real zombies who just enjoy inflicting pain and suffering on those who have supported the United States since Reagan? <u>Are they not the ones who ran this train off the cliff with deregulation</u> and other policies that encouraged spending like a drunken sailor when they felt they could get by with it? Are they not the ones who ran up a $12 trillion debt on our credit cards and those of our children and grand children even before the Democrats/Obama came into office? Are they not the ones who tried to shut down the government last summer and <u>were responsible for the down grading of the government financial rating for the first time in history</u>? A most decidedly, YES! <u>Then why would anyone in their right minds want to vote for this WRECKING CREW to do it all over again when we have so much to lose the second time? It's GREED - GREED OVER PEOPLE - (GOP)</u>!

We all, every one of us, <u>saw that movie before complete with a Mr. Holmes in front of the screen with an automatic weapon pointing at us. We all saw and lived this movie before and we all know far too well how it came out</u>! 12 million plus jobs lost or sent overseas, salaries down 10 to 40%, 35 million homes in foreclosure, savings and retirements down 10 to 100%, net worth down 40%. <u>Why in HELL would anyone want to see that movie again</u>? Why in HELL would anyone <u>want to hire the movie maker, the director or the sponsors</u> to make the <u>totally predictable sequel</u> in ad nausea? We all know <u>how bad sequels turn out</u>! We need to keep the present **FIXING CREW** working on fixing the mess that the GOP created when they drove that train off the cliff! If we were in the train at the bottom of the cliff, would we trust the engineer to try to get the train back up on the cliff – particularly when he and <u>they did nothing in 4 years to help us get up that cliff</u>! They just kept cutting the towing cables! The only thing <u>they were concerned about during those four years was, our wife's and daughters, vagina and writing state laws to keep us</u>

<u>from voting in the 2012 and all future elections</u>! <u>Voter restrictive disfranchisement laws were the very top of their priorities next to destroying unions</u>! How did they accomplish all this? Because, by crashing the economy, <u>our well being</u> and sense of well being, they had us by the proverbial BALLS – vulnerable, desperate, anxious for better times and the overwhelming need to be finding a savior! <u>We already hired the savior</u> so now we must hire the team in the House & Senate to make the comeback team very effective in solving the rest of the problems THAT THEY, THE GOP, DELIBERATELY CREATED TO TAKE CONTROL OF OUR ENTIRE LIVES FOR THE NEXT CENTURY!

96   Note to President Obama   8/28/12

<u>This is extremely important now that the GOP Convn is starting and hopefully in enough time for you to get these videos and put them on the screen during a crucial prime time speech at your Convention next week! This shows Mitt Romney in his own words bragging about getting the maximum amount of dollars to bail out the Olympics & his Utah business buddies and how he will grab every last Federal dollar to bail out a failing Mass. if he should be so LUCKY as to gets elected as governor.</u>

http://www.youtube.com/watch?v=L9S2daN0Kn8&feature=youtube_gdata_player
http://www.youtube.com/watch?v=9ui-EGWz-Bw&feature=related

The first one is about the Olympics money and he brags a bit about getting all the Federal money he can to bail out Massachusetts. The second one is a better view of both talks that brags about getting Federal money more than ever before to bail out the Olympics and to get every last dollar from the Feds to bail out Massachusetts. <u>These</u> lead to a host of other videos as well.

After the videos are played, the speaker should then ask the question: "So <u>Mitt, you bailed Massachusetts out with Federal Dollars, so where are you going to get the dollars to bail out the United States, the GOP bankrupted in the past decade</u>"? From a $5 trillion tax cut for the rich? From China on our children and grandchildren's credit cards like before? From the middle & lower classes by cutting crucial programs that have helped them in hard times that the GOP created like now? It damn site better come from the rich 1% who benefited the most by their bankrupting of America! Their salaries went up 400% while the middle class went down 40%. That is a real tax increase on the middle class that the GOP refuses to talk about! I just wonder why in HELL that is!!

(Bain of your Life) by his own words will bring fire to the Dem base that will see his true colors for what they are. Greed. By the way, mafia bosses were great family men and cared deeply for their own families, wives, children with great compassion but you wouldn't want a mafia boss anywhere near the White House nor would you want them to run a country of struggling Middle Class!

Something just brought this to mind that may be extremely important in regard to all those voter suppression and voter ID laws that the GOP have been enacting all over the country to suppress voting by minorities, elders, disabilities etc. When people register to vote in almost every state and county in the country, they AUTOMATICALLY become subject to being called to jury duty in the county or federal courts. These jury duty laws are strictly enforced with severe penalties for non show or non performance. There are very few exceptions or excuses allowed to get out of the duty including the following! Disabilities are generally not allowed as an excuse to get out of jury duty. The idea is if you have been eligible and able to vote, you must be subject to jury duty requirements with few exceptions!

Those opposed to the new voter laws have stated that it is easier to buy a gun, kill someone or rob a bank than it is to get a new voter ID under these new laws. They also show that it is easier to be called up for the draft (when that was operable) than to get these new IDs to vote. My point goes something like this: If one <u>MUST SERVE ON A JURY AS THE RESULT OF SIMPLY HAVING REGISTERED TO VOTE</u> (AND PERHAPS VOTED AT SOMETIME) AND <u>IT IS GOOD ENOUGH FOR THE COURT SYSTEM TO REQUIRE THAT YOU MUST by law SERVE ON JURY DUTY WHEN CALLED UPON AS A RESULT OF THAT PREVIOUS REGISTRATION</u>, then there can be by that reason, no way TO KEEP PREVIOUSLY REGISTERED VOTERS FROM VOTING IN CURRENT AND FUTURE ELECTIONS! THE LAWS RELATED TO THAT PREVIOUS REGISTRATION ARE SO STRONG AS TO HAVE CRIMINAL AND JAIL TIME PENALTIES FOR FAILURE TO SERVE ON JURIES ONLY <u>ON THE BASIS OF A PREVIOUS & THEN VALID VOTER REGISTRATION!</u> IE, IF THE STATE AND COUNTY BY THE NATURE OF THAT PREVIOUS REGISTRATION IS SO CONVINCED THAT THEY CAN PROSECUTE AND SEND YOU TO JAIL FOR FAILURE TO APPEAR, THEN THEY, <u>THE STATE AND COUNTY ARE, BY THAT LAW, ASCERTING THAT YOU ARE A DULY REGISTERED AND VALID VOTER</u> – IE. NO FURTHER ACTIONS REQUIRED! CONTRARILY, IF THE NEW VOTER LAWS ARE EFFECTIVE, IT THROWS THE ENTIRE COURT JURY SYSTEM OUT THE WINDOW AS EVERYONE CAN THEN CLAIM THAT THEY HAVE NO RESPONSIBILITY TO THE STATE OR COUNTY TO SERVE ON A JURY AS THEY HAVE BEEN DEEMED INELIGIBLE TO VOTE BY THE NEW STATE LAWS. <u>IT DESTROYS THE VERY EFFECTIVENESS OF ALL JURY LAWS!</u>

URGENT BEFORE CONVENTION THURSDAY NIGHT TALK!!!!! At DNC convention when you speak, you should have an empty chair occupied invisibly by GW Shrub. Your conversation could go something like: "What, they didn't

Invite you to the last two RNC conventions"? Why? You were the Last GOP president! Oh, You took a $5trill Dem created surplus and spent thru it to a $12trill deficit before I was elected? Oh! What? You rushed to two wars, one useless, needless and put the $3trill cost on our children's, grandchildren's and great grandchildren's credit cards and forced me thereby to put it on the budget creating a more visible deficit. Oh, that's bad for sure! What? When we still had the Dem created $5trill surplus, you justified a $3trill tax cut for the rich 1% to kind of fix things while things were solvent and now since, you created the worst depression since the 30's. Oh, I can see why they didn't want you at the conventions! What? There's more? You also created the worst depression in a century and caused 0.8 million job loss per month so that we ended up with at least 12 million unemployed before Barack was elected. Boy, the GOP was bad for America, weren't they? No wonder they didn't want to see you anywhere near the Convention!!! Oh God, no, there's more? Really? You deregulated Wall street and let their Greed and reckless irresponsible ways to destroy the world economies including ours?! No wonder your chair is empty. I frankly don't blame them! You and they and the GOP seem to be the worst enemies of America since 911. It's a good thing that we were able to take over in 2009 and turn around this mess that you created! We've not only created 4.6 million jobs since stopping your hemorrhaging job loss that could have gone to at least 15 million. You know, I'm glad that you chose to join our convention since they didn't want you at theirs. <u>You have spoken truth to their Greed for Power and have set their record straight. Etc</u>. You can add much more I'm sure!!

Notes to President Obama   9/17/12

FIRST OF ALL, CONGRATULATION ON A TRULY GREAT CONVENTION – IT KNOCKED THE GOP OUT OF THE PARK INTO NEVER, NEVER LAND! NOT TO DIMINISH ANYONE ELSE NOW BUT HOW LONG HAVE I BEEN TELLING YOU TO GET <u>CLINTON ON MESSAGE</u> AND HAVE HIM <u>GO TO BAT FOR YOU AND THE DEMOCRATIC PARTY AND TO TOUT YOUR ACCOMPLISHMENTS</u>! HE CAN SAY THINGS THAT NEITHER YOU or JOE CAN SAY FOR YOURSELVES! HE CAN <u>BE AN ADVOCATE</u> THAT CAN <u>TELL IT LIKE IT IS</u> WHEN FOR YOU TO SAY THE SAME THING <u>WOULD APPEAR TO BE SELF SERVING</u>! YOU NEED TO GET HIM OUT ON THE CAMPAIGN TRAIL ON A REGULAR BASIS AND HAVE HIM TELL THE WHOLE STORY ABOUT HOW THE GOP (ReCorpiCONs) HAVE <u>NEVER EVER BEEN</u> FOR THE MIDDLE CLASS, WE THE PEOPLE OR A GOVERNMENT THAT <u>TRULY SERVES AMERICA IN THE BEST POSSIBLE WAY TO MAKE IT THE MOST POWERFUL, COMPETITIVE NATION ON EARTH! THEY ARE, THEN AND NOW, ONLY FOR THE 1%ers AND CORPORATIONS</u>!

When Clinton spoke, I kept thinking that Joe would speak next or perhaps I had missed it. It wasn't until the next night that I learned that Joe was going to speak that night before President Obama. I thought, oh God, this, after Clinton, could be a huge let down. (Sorry Joe, not because I lost faith in you, but you know what it is like <u>following two dogs and a cute cat act</u> when you are the comic act that follows.) Hell, <u>you belted that talk right out of the park</u> and made the ReCorpiCONs very nervous that they truly had nothing to say to help America! All they could talk about is "How bad Obama has been for America"! BULL CRAP! You truly restored my long time faith in you as a speaker, statesman, a man of the people & <u>someone this Country desperately needs for not only this recovery but for the long term as well</u>! Oh, God, I thought, now Obama has to follow your "out of the park" speech! Well, Hell, he belted it out of the park as well. WELL DONE, WELL DONE ALL OF YOU – EVERYONE THAT SPOKE AT THE DNC CONVENTION! CUDOS TO ALL!

THE RNC CONVENTION LAYED THERE LIKE A <u>TURD DROPPED IN A MOST INAPPROPRIATE WAY</u>! AN ALL WHITE CROWD WAS <u>SOMEHOW SUPPOSED TO REPRESENT WE THE PEOPLE AND THE MIDDLE CLASS OF THESE UNITED STATES</u>! <u>WHAT AN OBVIOUS JOKE</u>! THE DNC CONVENTION ON THE OTHER HAND WAS <u>FILLED WITH A RAINBOW OF PEOPLE ALL ENJOYING LIFE TO THE FULLEST EVEN IN HARD TIMES</u>! I saw a myriad of faces that should have been, by character lines and wrinkles, sad, tired, discouraged and disillusioned by trauma, stress and economic catastrophes brought upon them by the ReCorpiCONs and the GOP party. Instead, I saw a diverse crowd that was eager, happy, full of life, full of hope and genuinely enjoying the life that they had been dealt and were sure that if they elected you and all the other needed Democrats to congress, they would again be on track for the American Dream that the ReCorpiCONs deliberately took away from them <u>according to plan</u>! <u>WHAT A STARK, OBVIOUS, CONTRAST</u>! To look at the Republicans as a group like that, you simply see sourly, stubborn, sad, unrelenting, regulating, judgmental and <u>'holier than thou'</u> people <u>who have not truly enjoyed one day of their entire lives without feeling guilty about it</u>!

102   Again, what a total joke, except the jokes on them! And Paul Ryan, who is trying to <u>sell the same snake oil</u> that the conservatives sold to Greece, Italy, Spain and Ireland is trying to make it seem that if we don't do the <u>same snake dance on our economy</u>, we will be just like Greece. Well, Duh! Who would know that better than the same crowd that did it to Greece, Italy, Spain and Ireland? These cats are the ones who brought all this trauma to the United States as well as a large part of the world & want to somehow blame it on the "up crowd" that is trying to get America up out of the ditch! <u>Shove it</u>!

Let's face facts! The ReCorpiCON party is the party of NO, Obstruction, decimation, <u>down grading of the might and power of these United States</u> and its faith and credit in the world! So where in Hell, did they suddenly become the party of concern for the middle class they destroyed or of the plight that they put the middle class into during the past generation! Where in hell was the "ALLIGATOR TEARS" concern for WE THE PEOPLE in the past four years? By the way, next term, Obama will be a truly one term President so there should be no wrangling about trying to get him out! Since they are now on record of being FOR THE PLIGHT OF THE MIDDLE CLASS AND JOBS, THEN THEY SHOULD HAVE NO TROUBLE STEPPING UP TO THE PLATE AND PASSING LEGISLATION GOOD FOR ALL OF AMERICA. They truly are the "GREED OVER PEOPLE" PARTY and the anti-people party. <u>Fight against the entire GOP not just the smiling Max Headroom</u>! It takes a <u>desperate scum bucket</u> to dance a <u>political jig</u> on the graves of four slain American diplomats! (Bain of your Life) truly has no soul or character at all! <u>How can governments ever trust him</u>?

Note to President Obama   9/21/12

Well, it seems that (Bain of Your Life) is continually shooting himself in the foot. The man is so dumb that he thinks that when he is in his "country club" environment that whatever he says to "friends" remains in the club! This is a political campaign, DUH! He made such a deal about "writing off 47% of America because they pay no income taxes and are totally dependent upon the government and since they pay no taxes would not be interested in tax cuts. Conclusion he made is they would automatically vote for Obama! They are dependant!

Hey, (Bain of Your Life), I have news for you.! You and your 1% friends are part of the 47% because you and many of them DO NOT PAY INCOME TAXES! You only pay capital gains taxes – if you don't somehow shelter them off shore. What is more, you are part of the largest, by far most expensive, government welfare program ever – huge tax cuts and special tax breaks and loop holes fitted to the "needs" of only the 1%ers. What is more, this giant government "welfare" program has ABSOLUTELY NO WORK REQUIREMENT! You are therefore a huge part of what you HATE ABOUT THE SO CALLED 'Obama' SOCIALIST AMERICAN GOVERNMENT! So start paying up dead beat. It is now time to pay the piper since you have been dancing the Royal dance so well for all these years!

Now, to Obama's comments some years ago about re-distribution of the wealth that (Bain of Your Life) is trying to make so much hay about! It's simple, which would you rather have, the Obama plan or the Romney GOP plan? The GOP plan is taking every last dime and nickel from the American Middle Class that they have worked a lifetime to earn by actually having a job and working and <u>re-distributing it UP to the top 1%</u> - who by the way did not earn it! In the past generation, the middle class income and net worth, by this GOP plan, has gone down some 20%-40% while the top 1% "salaries" and net worth have gone up some 200% – 400%! So if you were a reasonable person, which one makes more sense to provide for a Government BY & FOR WE THE PEOPLE and a growing and prosperous, powerful Nation? It would certainly not be the GOP plan! Never vote GOP again!

Again, I must point out a fact the GOP would like everyone to ignore or forget. The class warfare was started as far back as Reagan by the GOP and has been waged very effectively in the back ground ever since. So when they call you and the Democrats out for "starting" a class warfare, you might just point out that we didn't start this war nor are we propagating it but are merely the messengers and reporters of it and it's so far totally disastrous effects on the economy and the status of the middle class! They are truly the biggest hypocrites and Obfuscators of all time! (Bain of Your Life) has been on so many sides of every issue, it's like being on every side of a Rubik's cube – that simply just doesn't work and is not solvable!. His campaign is in such a destructive mode that even the Higgs Boson "GOD's particle" could not save it! (Bain of your life) is so self destructive that we should sneak him into the Taliban as a "secret weapon" and end the war in just a matter of months! <u>His campaign is on such a death spiral that the GOP has already written an eulogy for it and is right now digging the deep grave</u>!

We are now in need of removing every disastrous TeaBagger house member. If you ran a corporation and hired 63 people with staffs and offices, that did so little for the corporation as that group has done for the United States, <u>they would all be out on the street with all their belongings in a matter of minutes</u>. Keep in mind, <u>they and their staffs are all being paid by US the people of these United States</u> and they are DEAD BEATS! They are actually worse than just dead beat, near do wells! <u>They have been actively working to destroy the great name, faith and credit of these United States</u>! If you hired 63 people and staffs that did that to the corporation that hired them, they would not only be out on the street with all their belongings, <u>they would likely be facing court time, prosecutions and possibly jail time</u>! Yet these same 63+ people seem to think they can get by with "murder" working for the government that they profess to hate and claim is wasteful. <u>Guess who are the wasteful parts of that government! That is a message that has got to be sent out to all the Senate and House campaigns</u>.

We can no longer tolerate this destructive bunch in Congress and if you are going to get anything done next term, you must join the fight to get these louts and clouts out of office in November! THIS IS A MUST DO! They talk about one timers , they need to be the one timers!

I thought you were very presidential and statesmen like on Letterman. This was especially so when asked about the 47% comments. When I look into (Bain of Your Life)'s eyes, I see nothing but a vacuum and dastardly deeds! That image is somehow just not right for the President!

Note to President Obama   9/23/12

THIS IS TRULY THE BOTTOM LINE ABOUT THIS ELECTION!

America must have the greatest amnesia of the century! As a Republican all my life, when I look at even just the time of 2000 to 2008, it doesn't take me even 1 second to know that I would never ever vote for a Republican ever again - for all time! That response is burned into my psyche! It shouldn't take any convincing by a smooth talking politician; it shouldn't take any glad handing robot to change my mind; it shouldn't take a $1 billion in campaign funds/ads to change my mind – this GOP disaster is permanently imprinted upon my mind as something to avoid anytime and for all time! If anyone who lived through that period hesitates even 1 second to know which way to lean, they're 1%ers, corporations, just plain ignorant or on drugs the entire time! As a result, any vote, based on the GOP 2000-2008 disaster, should be 95% Democrats, 5% Republicans! How soon America forgets how bad a 12 million job loss is for them or how bad a monumental housing foreclosure crisis is for them or how bad it was to use our last dimes and nickels to bail out Wall Street that laid this holocaust on us or what a GOP generated $15 trillion in debt disaster is for America! Even one vote for anyone in the GOP is a vote for TRIPLING DOWN on this disaster in the next 4 or more years and is an ACT OF PURE INSANITY! This is not the only reason to vote for Obama and every Democrat in the House & Senate but IS A NECESSARY AND SUFFICIENT ONE INDEED! ONLY DISASTER CAN FOLLOW IF THIS NECESSARY AND SUFFICIENT CONDITION IS NOT HEEDED IN TIME!

People who truly want to get something for nothing are the Republicans! They want to use our money to make more money for themselves! They like government to provide every nature of advantages for them & their businesses but don't want to pay a dime for them! They want a "strong" army that protects them and their safe lives in America while providing $Billions in contracts for them! They want strong police and Fire departments to protect their businesses and fabulous homes and properties. They want an active rule of law, the best courts, jails and enforcement to litigate against all that would try to rule against them or their foibles in product and product liabilities. They want a strong central government to come bail them out when there is a natural disaster like Katrina or Hurricanes that run up the East Coast and destroy their Mansions. They want the government to pay for their children to attend the best private schools while letting public schools for all the rest of us to go to HELL! However, there's one thing that they don't want: to have to pay for any of these advantages they so grandiosely enjoy here in Amer. They want it all but want the middle class to pay for ALL OF IT! HUBRIS!

They want public and private Universities funded by government funded contracts to provide and develop new technologies to start new industries and competitive edged research for current industries to obtain a competitive superiority over each and every foreign competitor. They want these Universities to provide the best talent in the world for them to acquire and use without having to pay the cost to develop it themselves. They want the best schools, libraries, recreational facilities, arenas, parks and amenities that are prerequisites for companies to attract the best talent in the world to come to their city to work for them! <u>They want all this they have enjoyed for at least a century</u> but there is one thing <u>they absolutely do not want: to have to pay for them or "appear to have a need them"</u>! Guess who ends up paying for these and all other "common good" stimulants they so freely use? If it gets paid for, it is the middle class, that's now in so much financial hurt, that is forced to pay tor it & that can only mean higher taxes for them or for them to lose all the other services they need to survive! They want the middle class to pay for the Wall Street disasters when they screw up but do not share one dime of the billions they reap if successful! <u>Talk about the truly 'NEEDY' SOMETHING FOR NOTHING SOCIETY! IRONICALLY IT IS THE 1%, CORPORATIONS AND REPUBLICANS who're on welfare W/O work requirements</u>!

Everyone essentially tries to be frugal even in good times. However, in bad times, we all cut back on as many things as possible; trips to the store, lower heat, less A/C and cut back on food/pleasures. When we hit the bottom limit we try to add to income with moonlighting or other members getting jobs. That's just life we have become to know! When a millionaire cuts back—<u>Oh, I just made a funny</u>! You see, a millionaire could <u>EASILY FUND all the needs for 30 M/C families</u> and still have tons of discretionary <u>money left over to buy and sell Politicians and Elections</u>! So why is it that it is the <u>millionaires, the 1%ers, the rich corporations that are raising the</u> cry for lowering taxes so much? Why are they the ones trying to raise such rancor in the Middle Class about the need to

LOWER THE TAXES "for those poor, needy, strapped, stressed working people where the need may be real when the real goal is to reduce the taxes on those privileged even more than they have been lowered since the '50 – '60s (90%) or Reagan, (72%) or 35% now? It simply boils down to one thing and one thing only. It is called GREED! GREED FOR MONEY, POWER AND CONTROL! That's why they are called the (Greed Over People) party Oh yes, there's one other important thing: <u>it is because they can</u>! They have <u>bought</u> the politicians, House & Senate, the control of agencies that are crucial to their being able to get whatever they want and now they are for paying less taxes for themselves and having everyone else to pay a HELL of a lot more or lose everything that they need to get by in bad and good times! <u>We have got to stop them</u>! NEVER VOTE GOP EVER AGAIN! DO NOT EVER FALL FOR THE <u>PERFECT TRAP</u>. IF YOU DO YOU WILL BE 'FALLING' OFF THE CLIFF THAT THEY TOOK US OVER IN 2000 – 2008 -- ONLY THIS TIME ON STEROIDS! <u>WE HAVE EVERYTHING TO LOSE AND NOTHING TO GAIN BY SUCH A FOOLISH 'BY IN' TO THEIR GLIB PROPAGANDA!!</u>

<u>LOOK</u> AT EVERY ONE OF <u>THEIR STATEMENTS & PROPOSALS</u> AND LOOK FOR THE "WHY OF THE WHY" THEY'RE PUSHING SUCH A CONCEPT AND <u>YOU WILL BEGIN TO SEE THE TOTAL GOP AGENDA,</u> THAT THEY'VE PLANNED FOR AT LEAST TWO GENERATIONS, <u>OF THE TOTAL CAPTURE OF THE AMERICAN GOVERNMENT</u>! THAT IS PART OF THEIR <u>PERFECT TRAP AND THE ONE WE MUST ALL AVOID AT ALL COST!!</u> VOTE FOR DEMOCRATS BEFORE IT TOO LATE!! <u>A CENTURY IS A VERY, EVERY LONG TIME TO WAIT FOR THE GOOD TIMES AND THE HEY DAY OF AMERICA TO FINALLY COME BACK!</u>